Grey Fox Documents: 1

CLAUDE HARTLAND

THE STORY OF A LIFE:

FOR THE
CONSIDERATION
OF THE

MEDICAL FRATERNITY.

St. Louis, Mo.
1901.

CLAUDE HARTLAND

THE STORY OF A LIFE

*For the consideration of
the Medical Fraternity*

With a Foreword by

C. A. TRIPP

Grey Fox Press
San Francisco

Library of Congress Cataloging in Publication Data

Hartland, Claude, 1871–
  Claude Hartland : the story of a life.

  (Grey Fox documents ; 1)
  Hartland, Claude, 1871–   2. Homosexuals—
Missouri —Biography.   I. Title   II. Title: Story of a
life.   III. Series.
RC558.H36   1985   306.7'662'0924 [B]   85-12500
ISBN 0-912516-92-5
ISBN 0-912516-93-3   (pbk.)

Distributed by The Subterranean Company,
P.O. Box 10233, Eugene, OR 97440

DEDICATORY NOTE

To physicians, who have at heart the welfare of their fellow man, this little book is respectfully dedicated, with the one hope that it may furnish the key to a vast realm of human suffering, of which I find that they, as a body, are for the most part ignorant.

THE AUTHOR

CONTENTS

FOREWORD

Victorian times were especially hard on young gay men. And in the Victoriana of midwestern small-town America the situation was not better.

Fifty or a hundred years earlier (or simply farther west in the 1880s and 90s) a rough and ready frontier spirit with its naive ways and a looser social organization usually kept people from recognizing homosexual attachments. Thus many were inadvertently "permitted" to develop, even to continue, with relatively little danger of gossip or labeling of any kind. (Bat Masterson, for instance, could spend all his time with men, one in particular, with no risk of seeming or feeling exceptional, much less of coming across as in any way less masculine or "unnatural.")

But even in the rural environs of St. Louis a hundred years ago, there was already a tighter social structure than at the frontier, tight enough to hold and express puritanical codes with moral certitude. True, words like homosexual were not yet in common parlance, but there were firm religious notions concerning "natural law" to define what people thought was normal and abnormal, natural and unnatural. Such labels could be all the more punishing when self-applied by the average gay man who at first thought he was the only one to have homosexual urges and who, in any case, was unable to view them in any historical context.

Of course the main taboo, then as today, was on being a real or implied effeminate or "Uranist" (from the quaint nineteenth-century notion that men attracted to men were both as newly discovered and as out-of-this-world as the newfound planet Uranus). Effeminacy, or at least being something less than fully male—usually something in between maleness and femaleness—was implied ("intersexuality," "the third sex," etc.). Should a decidedly masculine man happen to be involved, then either he was merely pretending to be a real man ("letting his hair down" only in private), or else, as today, it was thought he must surely "be on top" in sex; perhaps he was merely responding to some circumstantial opportunity, and thus was not really homosexual at all.

Where any actual effeminacy existed, as with Hartland, the case seemed proved, with numerous ramifications and consequences. For one thing, elements of effeminacy were often intensified, first and foremost by being interpreted by the boy himself as an indication of some kind of impaired masculinity. Sometimes his very identity was thrown into question, much as a cliché of the time had it, "a woman in a man's body." Hartland didn't go that far, but at an early age he did reach out to conclude that his narrow waist and long fingers, even on his lanky six-foot frame, were "feminine."

While being effeminate in any way was certainly not socially favorable, by itself it was not necessarily disastrous. Neither of Hartland's uneducated parents nor his brothers, nor family friends seemed at all concerned with his sometimes girl-like ways. These were viewed simply as part of his particular disposition, no doubt as merely "a phase" anyway. No ipso facto assumptions needed to be made, nor were they made, about his later sex life.

These views might seem remarkably liberal even today. But if that were the case a hundred years ago, it was an accidental liberality, born less of any tolerance than of an understandable hesitance to bring down on the head of any still-innocent youngster the fierce rejection and moral righteousness that were instantly applicable to any man known to be sexually interested in men.

On the other hand, an abysmal general ignorance of homosexuality, no open discussion of it, and in any case few words to define it, often made approaches in those days easier to arrange and to carry out than would otherwise have been possible. One could invite a friend to spend the night (or the friend on the slightest pretext might invite himself into the same bed) with no suspicion or intent implied. Or from sheer affection, the same-sex object of one's admiration could sometimes be embraced, even kissed, with what was assumed at the time to be a platonic, entirely laudable emotion.

All this is found in Claude Hartland, together with punishing self-judgments for his having lewd, "unnatural" desires on the one hand, and on the other, many unstinting try-outs. He describes his own sexual disposition as being of "two perfectly distinct kinds: spiritual and animal." Wherever the animal rears its ugly head, he professes an exceptional amount of guilt, perhaps more than most others felt, even in those days. But are his frequent laments to be taken at face value, or are they partly intended to assuage judgmental readers? He does seem to have oscillated further and more often than most people between the emotional extremes of depression and of soaring spirits. And yet much of his running account has the pace and the joy of a nineteenth-century *Song of the Loon*.

Notable, too, is that throughout these various cross-currents, Hartland manages to sketch a remarkable picture of his life and times, one filled with a wealth of authentic detail which goes far beyond his own peculiarities. The images include all too familiar scenes, even how small-town doctors reacted a hundred years ago when approached for advice about his "condition" (their reactions are astonishingly close to those still found today among many practitioners). Both the doctors and the sometimes dire consequences of their advice are entertainingly, even hilariously described. It's interesting, too, that such things as the street-cruising and the style of individual pickups back then were so similar to their present-day equivalents.

The panorama of what one sees through the eyes and experiences of Hartland is made all the more impressive by his being an extraordinarily talented and perceptive writer. Often his descriptions even seem improved by his sometimes flowery Victorian language. But flowery or not, he time and again, often with very few words, proves remarkably adroit at using quick, incisive strokes and a dry wit to picture complex scenes in depth. In fact, the whole book is quick and short and to the point—to quite a few points, and we are lucky to have it.

C. A. TRIPP, PH.D.
Nyack, N.Y., May, 1985

PUBLISHER'S NOTE

We are indebted to Burton Weiss, who very kindly made available xerox copies of the rare first edition of Claude Hartland's *The Story of a Life* in his collection.

In the present resetting of the autobiography the original text has been faithfully followed, except for the silent correction of perhaps a dozen minor typographical errors. In several instances, words that seem to be missing are supplied in square brackets. In one case, on page 67, [flaunt] has been supplied as probably nearer the author's intent than the *flout* of the 1901 edition.

PREFACE

In the following chapters, appears the history of a being who has the beard and the well-developed sexual organs of a man, but who is, from almost every other point of view, a woman.

He has the delicate, refined tastes of a woman, and what is worse, her sexual desires for men.

Physically, he is a strange combination of male and female.

He has the hands, arms, and waist of a woman, while his shoulders, hips, lower limbs, and feet are those of a man.

All his natural inclinations are effeminate, and he has never felt one thrill of sexual desire for a female.

In this little volume he offers to the medical world the strange story of his own life, hoping that it may be a means by which other similar sufferers may be reached and relieved.

C. H.

INTRODUCTION

For the following chapters I offer no apology; neither do I wish to tax my reader's patience with a long list of excuses for the happenings recorded therein.

I wish merely to say that, however incredulous this story may seem to the natural man, I solemnly swear in the presence of Almighty God that it is true as truth itself.

I have not once offered an exaggerated description, but many times have I fallen short of language to express the intense feelings of pleasure or pain that have checkered my strangely wretched life.

I have never before written a book. I am neither rhetorician, logician, nor philosopher; and if I were all three combined, neither should show his face in this special little volume, which is not written for the edification or entertainment of its readers, but as a channel through which science may reach and relieve a certain class of individuals who live, suffer a hundred deaths, and die with their strange secret hidden away in their bosoms.

The very nature of the disease accounts for the general ignorance on the part of those who might relieve it.

To the natural man it is incomprehensible, unbelievable; and, as a general thing, the victim would rather suffer in silence than to seek relief at the risk of divulging his secret. Year after year the malady spreads.

In the last few years the list of suicides without apparent cause has swollen to alarming proportions.

Week after week, with the hope of finding relief, misalliances are made, hearts broken, lives wrecked and ruined, and the world wonders why.

As an explanation to a great part of this misery, and with the hope of relieving it in a measure, I have written the story of my own life, which is but a counterpart to thousands in our country and even in this city to-day.

It is not the product of a sudden impulse—far from it.

For several years I have been hesitating between duty and fear—duty to the thousands of such sufferers as myself, living and unborn, and fear of the reproach and scorn of the public should my secret become generally known.

The events recorded in the eleventh and twelfth chapters have decided the matter for me.

I know and love but few people in the world; am known and loved by fewer still. My life has ended.

All hope of peace and happiness in this world has faded forever, and my soul turns trustfully to the Great Beyond.

At any rate, the sacrifice can but be small; the result for good may be great. So have I reasoned and so have I written.

At the hand of my reader I seek no sympathy. I fear no condemnation. All I ask is a just and unprejudiced consideration of the following story, not for my sake, but for the sake of those who are suffering and may suffer the tortures of a life like mine, and I shall ever remain,

Most gratefully yours,

CLAUDE HARTLAND

THE STORY OF A LIFE

CHAPTER I

ANCESTRY, BIRTH AND EARLY CHILDHOOD

My ancestry, which I can trace with accuracy only three generations back, is characterized by nothing extraordinary along any line.

My mother came of an old Virginia family noted more for honesty, industry, and morality than for wealth; while my father descended from a southern family of greater financial importance, but with a much less practical idea of life.

My mother's people, so far as I can learn, were exceedingly practical and matter-of-fact, none of them in the least literarily inclined.

My grandfather on my mother's side was father of twelve children, six boys and six girls; my mother being the fourth child and second girl.

They were a very strong and long-lived race, but two of them having died younger than seventy-four years.

I have never learned that there was any nervous trouble of any account among my mother's people.

They all married when quite young and became parents of large families.

My mother's father, being a slave owner till the Civil War, was never forced to perform any manual labor, and my mother often speaks of his skill in ladies' work, such as sewing, knitting, mending, and even cooking. Most of his time was spent in this way, his wife caring but little for domestic affairs.

While he was strong and manly in appearance, I can but look to him as the source of my own trouble, for experience and observation have taught me that 'tis only the effeminate that turn so naturally to household pursuits.

He was a man of very strong likes and dislikes, seldom forgiving an injury, or forgetting a kindness. He was just himself and demanded justice of everyone else.

Among his children his word was law, but he was often influenced by his wife.

He was called eccentric by some, but I have not learned along what lines.

A description of him serves also as a description of my mother, for they were much the same in disposition.

My mother, though of medium stature, is strong, resolute, practical and naturally unforgiving; yet just, generous and sympathetic to a degree.

She loves her children with a strong motherly affection, and was never known to neglect her duty in the home, yet she is entirely free from any sentimental nonsense. I have never seen her kiss or fondle one of her children, but night after night have I known her to sit from sun to sun by the bedside of my invalid brother.

Like her father, her word in her home was law. She never refused a reasonable request, but when yes or no was spoken it was never recalled.

She seldom made an unconditional promise, but when she did, 'twas fulfilled to the letter.

She has a limited education and reads but little, yet she is far from being ignorant.

About thirty years after her marriage, when I was thirteen, she began to suffer considerably from nervousness, which lasted for several years, but she has entirely recovered and is now a strong woman at the age of seventy.

My father is the eldest of seven children, five boys and six girls.

As I have said before, my father's people were more literarily and less practically inclined than those of my mother; neither were they so strong physically, two sisters and a brother having died of contracted lung disease when comparatively young.

The remaining children have married and have families of their own.

From early boyhood my father cared nothing for the common pursuits of life, but turned his attention to his books and for a man of his day was superiorly educated.

He was a great lover of music and fine literature, and having a good voice and a finished education, he taught vocal music and English for over twenty years, after which he turned his attention to politics, in which he succeeded fairly well for eight or nine years, but finally withdrew to private life in the country.

In his younger days, so strong was his love for poetry that he would often relapse for hours into a thoughtful silence, during which he would compose verse after verse, and in the absence of paper would write them on his linen or the toe of his shoe.

His lines were always sad—always sweet and gentle; many of which he set to music and sang with a feeling which never failed to touch his listeners.

My mother, though a loving and dutiful wife, could neither understand nor appreciate these poetic sentiments, and being left so much to his own thoughts it was feared that his mind would suffer, and he was advised to leave them off.

This he did with many regrets and has never taken them up again, yet it is not hard to see that he is none the less a dreamer.

Such are the ancestors of which I am an offspring—a matter of fact mother, a spiritual, poetic father, without a trace of insanity or extreme nervousness on either side for generations back.

My father has one brother who is noted for his peculiarities, such as extreme sensitiveness and unstable character in general, but he is father of eight children, and as husband and father is above reproach.

I am sure he is a victim to some abnormal development or arrest of development, but I do not believe it is of a sexual nature.

The following is a true account of my own condition from birth to February 22, 1901.

As I told you before, I am not going to promise you Logic, Philosophy or Rhetoric, nor even good English at all times; but I do solemnly promise, with God as my witness, to give you truth—to tell you the events of my life, not as they would appear to the natural man, but as they appeared to me.

I do this for no reason other than that you may understand to what extent I am unnatural; that you may more clearly see how to assist some similarly unfortunate being who is not beyond the pale of human assistance.

I was born in the early spring of the year 1871, in a small railway town in the south.

The conditions surrounding my parents during the year prior to my birth were, so far as I have learned, of an uneventful and humdrum nature, giving no clew to my present condition.

As an infant I have never been told that I differed from others. It is said that I cried a great deal, but this would not be called a difference.

When I was four years old, I burned three of my fingers very severely, and my mother made for them three little cloth cases or stalls.

I do not remember the burn in any way, but I clearly recall the stalls and how I loved them after my burns were well.

This is as far back as my memory extends. From that time I was not like other children.

We moved out on a farm the following fall and 'twas there that my life really began.

It was a small rough farm, shut in on all sides by cedar woods and forest trees. Days and even weeks passed without my seeing an unfamiliar face, but I gave this no thought, for I was not five years old, and besides I liked to be alone.

Young as I was I would often steal away from my brothers and go out into the woods, sit or lie down in the shade, and dream for hours.

I would sometimes fall asleep and 'twas then that my dreams were sweetest.

Again I would gaze far away into the heavens and imagine I saw all kinds of beautiful beings and things.

If the sky was clouded I could see the clouds shape themselves into dogs, horses, human beings and white-winged angels.

Every bird, tree and flower had a meaning for me. I loved the solitude of the woods. I loved the songs of the birds, the sighing of the winds and I was happy.

Sometimes strange fears would come over me and I would weep, but no one knew, and my fear was soon forgotten in some new joy.

Even at the age of five I was sensitive in the extreme and shrank with horror from causing any one or anything pain.

I say "anything," for I felt that the trees and flowers suffered and rejoiced as I did. I often refused to pluck a flower for fear it would be grieved to leave its friends. If one were accidentally broken, I would kneel down beside it and weep in sympathy.

At times I dreaded to walk lest I should kill some helpless insect on the ground.

At such times my sympathy extended much further than for the creature in question. I pictured to myself its little ones at home awaiting its return day after day, yet waiting in vain.

I saw the friends of the unfortunate heartbroken and sad, searching woods and fields for the missing loved one.

I imagined their terrible grief when they found the crushed body, and it was then that I viewed myself as a cruel monster, disregarding the sufferings of the helpless.

If I found an insect of any kind in distress, I never failed to relieve it if possible. I have often run narrow risks and soiled my clothing terribly in trying to rescue some unfortunate creature that had fallen into a pond that was near my home.

I cared for nothing that boys of my age usually like. My only toys were dolls, and my playmates the birds and flowers.

When I was not out in the woods dreaming, I was sitting by my mother or sister, either sewing or watching them with all interest.

This desire to sew grew upon me till my mother, becoming annoyed at my constant demand for needles, thread and so forth, refused to give them to me.

I knew it was useless to repeat the request, and one day when I could find no needle, I got an old fork, made holes in the goods and ran the thread through.

From that time I was not refused a needle, and many were the dolls' hats, dresses, etc. I planned and constructed.

With my dolls, my dreams and my sewing, I lived till I was eight years of age, when my perverted nature took on new and graver elements.

I was rushing on into ruin, but I did not know it.

If my parents could have seen the dark future in store for me,

I might have been saved, but they did not understand. They thought of me only as a peculiar child and nothing more.

These are delicate matters, it is true, and unpleasant to contemplate, but they are *facts* all the same, graver than delicate, and sadder than unpleasant—facts that must be seriously considered by the mothers and fathers of our country; otherwise, I *tremble* for the future of society.

But before a fact can be considered, it must be presented.

It would not be well for me to attempt a direct communication of said facts for many reasons; first, I should not be believed; again I should be arrested as an escaped lunatic, held up before the curious eyes of the public as a "nine days'" wonder, and then thrust into the dungeon of disgrace and forgotten, without having accomplished a single aim.

For ten years I have thought the matter over, and have arrived at the conclusion that it is mainly through the physicians that this information may be successfully disseminated and the progress of the malady checked.

I am led to this conclusion from a knowledge of the implicit confidence which most parents impose in the wisdom of their family physician.

I feel sure that if Dr. B. had told my parents of the danger I was encountering, my life would have been different; but he did not know it himself, nor do I believe that he (like many other general practitioners) had any knowledge of the existence of a disease like mine.

I write this little book, hoping that it may lead the physicians to give more thought to this all-important subject, and that they, in turn, may open the eyes of the laity in such a way as to check the spread of this worst of all diseases.

I am no physician, neither am I especially gifted intellectually; but I believe that my experience and sufferings have given me a knowledge along certain lines that the profoundest neurologist can never acquire from study alone.

So with the physicians' scientific achievements, which are beyond my reach, combined with my personal experiences, which can never be theirs, I believe a great step can be taken toward relieving such sufferers as myself, and preventing the existence of others yet unborn.

    Will you help me?

    If I could make you understand how numerous we are, and how intense our sufferings, every tongue would utter *"Yes."*

CHAPTER II

As I grew older more of my time was given to my dolls and my sewing, but my rambles and day-dreams were not neglected.

I had dolls of all kinds, and at the age of nine I had gained such proficiency with my needle that my dolls' costumes were a wonder to all who saw them.

I used large boxes for their houses and had furniture of every description made from the wood of cigar boxes. I was not so good at carpentering as at dress making, but it had to be done, and I got along fairly well.

Many were the marriages and deaths in my doll families, and many the tears shed upon such occasions.

When a doll was broken beyond repair she was supposed to be dead, and then followed the making of coffin and shroud, the digging of a grave, the funeral and burial, and lastly, the erecting of a handsome monument, which was usually of wood painted white.

After the burial every surviving member of the deceased doll's family went into deep mourning for twelve days, each day being considered a month.

At the end of the twelfth day a little white was added to their costumes, and for the next six days they were in second mourning. At the end of this time they again appeared in colors and all went well till the Death Angel returned.

Being naturally of a serious and gloomy disposition, I, in this way, soon developed an intense interest in all scenes of sorrow and suffering and was never happier than when allowed to attend a real funeral and burial.

I cannot explain my feelings upon such occasions.

I felt no pleasure at seeing others suffer, but at such times there was in my heart a sweet feeling of sympathy that filled my soul with an unspeakable satisfaction.

After attending a few real funerals, I at once became an undertaker. Coffins of all kinds were made, varnished and lined with the greatest care, and kept in readiness for dead dolls, fowls, and even animals of a manageable size.

I was never tempted to break a doll, or kill an animal or fowl for the sake of burying it, for I have but little destructiveness in my nature, but daily were my visits to the poultry coops to see if some unfortunate chick had not passed away during the night.

A few such burials necessitated the making of a hearse, which was done at once. To this was hitched "Tolbert," a little black dog belonging to my sister, and the pet of the whole family.

My happiness was complete.

The days were all too short for my funerals, my dolls, and my dreams. A year passed swiftly by, when at last a cloud appeared.

One evening after supper, when we were gathered around the front door in the moonlight, my mother told me that I must start to school.

My heart was broken, but I never thought of remonstrance, so the following Monday morning I, with two or three of my brothers, was sent to a public school in the country.

I was nearly ten at this time, but I could not read.

The first day in school brought me to realize how different I was from other boys of my age. My brothers got along fairly well, but I was miserable.

I longed to be back among my dolls and coffins.

I was shocked rather than amused at their noisy sports and refused to join them.

I was laughed at, called a "girl-boy," and I was only too glad when the teacher called us in.

As I had never known anything but perfect obedience at home, I got along nicely with my teacher and learned very well.

No one seemed to care for me at first but a little black-eyed girl, who seemed to feel sorry for me, and soon after I entered school she came up to me and began a conversation.

I loved her from that moment and I love her still, though she has been married for years and now has children of her own in school.

After our first talk we were constantly together during rests, and often during study hours I would deliberately walk over to her desk and sit down beside her.

At first every one teased us, but that we were in love soon became a matter of course to everyone but me, and nothing more was said of it.

I did not know the meaning of the word love. My love for her was just such as I felt for my dolls.

I have never in my life felt one thrill of the love that the natural man claims to feel for the opposite sex.

Day after day my little friend and I became more attached to each other, and I was soon a general favorite among the girls and not disliked by the boys.

My evenings at home were now spent either in playing with my dolls or cutting out pictures from magazines, floral catalogues and so on, for my little playmate at school; and various were the kinds of "pretties" that we exchanged during our long and fast friendship.

Saturday was a very busy day for me. There were dead fowls to bury; new coffins to make; washing, ironing and sewing to be done, for the doll family, besides an unusually large collection of trinkets to be got together for my Monday's gift to Ella (that was her name). We were now constantly together. We sat together during recitation, and if one of us failed to recite properly and was "turned down," the other intentionally missed the next word that we might not be separated.

We sat in the class with our arms about each other just as though we had been brother and sister and nothing was thought of it.

She was the brightest pupil in school.

I learned fairly well, but not nearly so well as she, and I have often seen a cloud of mingled sorrow and affection on her face when my recitations failed to reach her idea of perfection.

Sometimes during rest she would try to teach me my lesson, but I preferred to talk about dolls or to look at pictures, so her instruction seldom amounted to much.

With my little friend at school and my playthings at home, the time passed swiftly away till I was eleven years old, when a new and stronger desire than I had hitherto felt, took possession of me—a desire to dress in female attire.

Being unable to see the evil results, I followed this new inclination to the last extreme.

Whenever I had the time to spare, I would steal off to my sister's apartments, and donning her best gown, would walk up and down the room for hours, holding up my skirts and putting on all sorts of effeminate airs.

My sister, who loved me devotedly and indulged me along every possible line, made but little remonstrance, and in return I was very careful not to soil her clothing.

The desire grew into a passion, and I indulged it to the utmost limit.

Not being satisfied with my sister's clothes, I begged old skirts of her, which I cut and made into garments of my own, the waists of which I could never get tight enough to please me. This of course called for a corset, the wearing of which gave me the keenest delight, yet I could never draw it tight enough.

I remember at one time to have drawn a metal belt so tightly that I could not walk across the floor, my body swaying to and fro for want of support.

Hats and dresses of all kinds were made and worn with greatest pride, and when thus attired I felt that I was in my natural element.

I felt no shame at being seen in female attire and would have worn it all the time had I been allowed.

My features, form, voice and tastes were those of a female, and I felt out of place in boy's clothes.

I had neither taste nor ability for masculine pursuits, but was an expert at women's work of almost every kind. I could sew, knit, embroider, quilt and so forth, but I was never a very good cook.

So effeminate was I in every way that I was not expected to do any out of door work of any kind, and if I were called upon to assist my brothers out of doors, I knew nothing whatever about the work.

I simply hated any kind of coarse labor, and all I was expected to do was to bring in wood from the yard. This I often did directly after breakfast in order to have it off my mind.

In this way my muscular development was entirely neglected, and though I have nearly always been in perfect physical health, I have almost no muscle at all.

Perhaps this would be a good place to describe my personal appearance.

I am exactly 6 feet tall, weigh 120 pounds, with fair complexion, rather light hair and peculiarly colored eyes—between a light blue and a dingy greenish gray.

I wear a number 7 hat, 7 glove, 6 shoe, 14 shirt and collar, 33 coat, and my trousers measure only 27 inches in the waist and 36 inches in the leg.

My waist tapers like that of a woman, and I can easily contract it to 20 inches.

My hand is very slender and shaped exactly like a woman's.

There was never any natural change in my voice as I grew up, and I talked and sang like a woman. Being very sensitive along this line, I, at the age of twenty-one, employed an elocutionist to tone my voice down to a masculine pitch; which, with his assistance and constant practice, has become second nature, and I no longer have a woman's voice.

Even now when I sing my voice is that of a woman, and I never sing in public on that account.

I remember one occasion in particular, and I think it was the last time I ever sang for the entertainment of others.

A crowd of young people had gathered in a social way, and I was called upon to sing. I disliked to do so, but as almost every one present was acquainted with my effeminate voice, and I felt that I should not be subject to ridicule, I finally consented.

There was one young lady present who was never happier than when offering a disguised insult to some one in such a gentle and sweet manner, that the less suspecting and sensitive would have taken it as a rare compliment.

When I had finished the first stanza and the chorus, I turned to the listeners and asked to be excused from further attempt.

Then followed the usual round of flattery and solicitations to continue that are customary upon such occasions.

I glanced at "Miss Sarcasm," who had not yet expressed herself.

A strange smile, that I felt sure forboded embarrassment for me, was playing about her lips.

I did not know what it meant, but I knew that *something* was coming, and I made up my mind to return it if I could possibly do so in a passably civil way.

When everyone had finished, and she had, in her "woman's" way, secured the attention of all present, she said, in the sweetest tones you ever heard: "Oh, Mr. H., don't think of stopping! You have such a sweet voice! You sing *exactly* like a girl."

Well, I was so angry that I fear I should have been tempted to strike her had she been less repulsive to my sense of touch; instead, I merely said: "Thank you, Miss ——, I esteem that the greatest of all compliments, but do you know that there is a reason for my having the voice of a girl?"

"No," she replied, everything forgotten in her intense curiosity; "do tell us the reason."

I waited till I had everyone's attention, then coolly replied: "Why, my mother was a woman."

With this I turned again to the piano, and began to sing, but, judging from the uproar in the room, no one heard my song.

When I had finished, her face was still a deep crimson, but she did not venture another compliment.

This reply was not original, but I don't think any one present had heard it before; anyway it served to extricate me from a most embarrassing predicament.

As I have said before, I don't think I ever sang in public again.

Any reference to my effeminacy stings me keenly even now, and I do all I can to prevent the discovery of the truth.

I wear my clothing as loose as possible; and now, since my voice and walk have changed, my hands are about the only distinguishing feature visible.

I have a full beard now and a rather heavy mustache, due I suppose to constant shaving, for at eighteen my face was as soft and smooth as a girl's.

I have often wondered how my parents could have been so blind to the results as to allow me to completely neglect my physical development, but such was the case, and even now they have never dreamed of my sufferings.

While I am convinced that I was never a natural child, by proper early training, mental and physical, I might have been able to subdue these terrible impulses and finally to have overcome them; but 'tis useless to reflect; there is no rescue now.

I, individually, am helpless, powerless; but that others may be saved from such a fate, I place this little book into the hands of those who should best know how to use it.

CHAPTER III

THE MIDNIGHT CURSE

(11 to 13)

Until I was past eleven years of age my life was as simple, innocent and pure as a life could be.

Until I started to school I don't think I had ever heard half a dozen vulgar or profane words.

I had had no sexual experiences or desires of any kind, and did not even know of their existence; but at the age of eleven the wearing of female attire began to be accompanied by violent erections and an uneasy longing to which I could not give expression.

I was known as a very peculiar but good child. I had a violent temper, but it was seldom aroused, as I was almost always alone.

I had a great dislike for any form of cruelty, and lying or dissembling in any way I could not tolerate.

I had a very sensitive conscience, which up to this time had caused me but little pain.

Hitherto my life had been all happiness and sunshine, ignorance and bliss; but the clouds were beginning to gather, and one summer night at 12 o'clock, when I was past eleven years of age, the storm burst forth in all its fury. At this time a cousin of mine, a tall, well-developed young man, with dark eyes, hair and mustache, was visiting my eldest brother.

The day had been very warm, and that evening after supper he and my brother went to a river near by for a swim.

It was 12 o'clock when they returned, and I was asleep on my lounge in my mother's room. I slept well, but not soundly, and their entrance and conversation awoke me.

They were discussing the sports of the evening, to which

I listened with indifference till my cousin spoke of standing upon a bluff and jumping into the water for a dive. This was all I heard.

The blood rushed to my face, my head throbbed violently, and it seemed that my eyes were bursting from their sockets.

An erection immediately followed, and I longed to spring from my bed, clasp my cousin in my arms, kiss his lips, and give full expression to this new passion that was simply devouring me.

I longed to have seen him without his clothing, to have felt his warm flesh with my hand, to have clasped his naked form to my own in one endless embrace.

Oh! if I could only have died that night in my little bed; but no, I must live—live to suffer a thousand deaths on earth, and then be swept into a strange uncertain future beyond the grave.

The boys soon left the room, but I could not sleep.

The manly form and handsome face of my cousin were ever before me.

I closed my eyes, but I saw him still.

I covered up my head with my pillow, but I could not shut him out, and 'twas only after I was utterly exhausted that I fell into a feverish slumber, to awaken in the morning a miserable victim to this strange, unnatural passion.

When he appeared at breakfast the blood again rushed to my face, and I could scarcely keep from springing into his arms.

Soon after breakfast he took his leave for home. It broke my heart to see him go, and I have never been happy since.

The demon of an unnatural lust had entered my soul, to blight and ruin all that was noble and good.

I went out into the woods, but I was not happy.

The same sun was shining, but it now seemed murky and dim. The birds were singing still, but the music had fled from their songs.

I pined several days for my cousin, and cared but little for play of any kind. I was very cross and unkind to my brothers, and my mother thought that I was sick.

I soon found that my passion was not confined to him alone,

for I felt the same for every handsome and well-developed man I saw.

I had never done anything wrong at this time, yet a feeling of guilt had settled upon me and I could not shake it off.

I continued in school and loved Ella as much as ever, but I never felt good enough for her again.

Often when playing in the woods this desire for my own sex would come over me and make me miserable.

It was upon one of these occasions that I accidentally learned to relieve myself.

As it was not what I was seeking and gave me only temporary relief, I did not follow it closely enough to injure my health, not averaging over three or four times a week.

Soon after this my life became filled with strange desires, fears and coincidences that I can neither understand nor explain. I merely relate them, and leave my readers to account for them as they choose. All old desires were present still, but they had grown morbid and feverish.

I loved my dolls and funerals more than ever, but I was not nearly so happy with them.

Now, when I made my rounds in search of dead fowls to bury, I was disappointed and half-angry at not finding any, yet I was never once tempted to do them violence.

At this time I owned a beautiful yellow cat and loved it very much.

I didn't think I was impressed that it was going to die soon, but I decided to make it a nice coffin and shroud and have it ready in case of emergency.

Forthwith a beautiful coffin was made, painted brown, varnished, and lined with pure white.

This was done on Saturday. Monday I had to go to school, so I cut out the shroud, carried it with me, and stealing off to the woods alone, worked on it at rest and at noon.

Of course I accounted to Ella for my necessary absence.

I think I finished the work Tuesday at noon, and that evening the coffin, containing the shroud, was placed in a closet to await the death of my cat.

The same evening my father and mother were going out for

a walk, and I was to accompany them.

I ran out into the hall to get my hat, which I had left upon a settee. I found my cat on the settee, and when my hand touched her she mewed piteously as though she were in pain, but being in a hurry, I gave it but little thought.

The next morning, however, I found her in the same place cold and dead.

I was simply overcome with horror, not so much at the loss of my pet as at her dying on the very day her coffin and shroud were finished.

My mother and brothers laughingly told me that I had caused her death, which I denied, but in my heart I feared it was true.

The next day I stayed out of school, and laid her to rest in the promiscuous burial ground, but it was months and even years before I learned to look lightly upon this strange coincidence.

Shortly after this, my mother, being an expert with her needle, was making a pair of trousers for a certain Mr. C., with whom I was in love.

My sister, who was helping her, worked the buttonholes in the wrong piece, ruining it entirely.

I asked her for the ruined piece, intending to keep it as a memento of my beloved friend; but as soon as it was given me a feeling of awful fear came over me. I felt that if I kept it, something dreadful would happen to Mr. C., and I did not get rid of this strange impression till the piece was burned up.

I was often impressed with an idea that, unless I performed some trivial act, terrible results would follow; for instance, unlesss I touched a certain branch of a certain tree my mother would die.

Of course all this seems perfectly ridiculous to the natural man, but to me it was most real.

I remember one day, while out in the yard alone, to have had my future life portrayed to me in all its darkness and sorrow. I do not know how the impression came, but I was made to realize that there would never be another ray of sunshine in my miserable life, and I shrank from the future with such horrible dread that I resolved to commit suicide.

Securing a rope, I started to the barn, determined to hang myself. On my way I met my mother, who, thinking I intended to make a swing, took the rope from me and carried it into the house.

I do not know that I should have had the courage to take my life even if my mother had not interfered, but my intentions at that time were sincere.

I have never been tempted to do so again, nor do I think I ever shall, for I am sure my worst suffering is over.

When I was about twelve years old a strange impression came over me and completely took possession of my mind for several weeks.

I was impressed that some day I should become the possessor of many small babies, and that I should at once begin to prepare clothes for them. I was not particularly impressed that the children would be mine, but I felt that I would have charge of them and their wardrobe.

I neglected my dolls for some time, and babies' garments of all kinds were made and hidden away in drawers and boxes. My mother and sister found them and questioned me closely, but I did not give them very satisfactory replies; and they decided that I had made them for a gift to a small baby in the neighborhood, and had not had a chance to present them.

As far as I was concerned, this was a very satisfactory view for them to take, and nothing more was said of the matter. After their discovery I decided to bury the garments, but before this was done the impression left me, and I have never felt it since.

I was also subject to strangely vivid dreams, many of which came true to the letter.

I remember one morning at breakfast my mother announced that the pantry key was lost and could not be found. Everyone was questioned concerning it and cautioned to look for it during the day.

Night came and it had not been found. I looked upon its loss as a most serious matter, and when I retired I resolved to dream of its whereabouts.

I went to sleep thinking only of the missing key, and

during the night I had an unusually vivid dream. I could see a small hole in the pantry floor, and on looking through it I saw the string attached to the key.

When I awoke in the morning and told my dream, everyone laughed at me; but I did not mind that, for I knew they would be convinced as soon as the door was opened and I was allowed to examine the floor. The lock, which worked with a spring, had been fastened after the key was lost, and before the door could be opened a staple had to be drawn.

As soon as this was done, I ran inside, and finding the hole in the floor, I looked into it, and there was the key just as I had seen it in my dream.

This seemed rather strange to my people, but as they were not inclined to superstition, they decided that it was merely a "happen so," and there the matter dropped.

Many such happenings have filled my life from early childhood on, but I will not weary my reader with too many of them.

Two years had now elapsed since this mysterious curse had fallen upon me, and I was constantly growing worse. Day by day my perverted nature was becoming more and more perverse, and I was being hurried unwittingly into ruin without any effort to save myself.

CHAPTER IV

THE DEATH OF TOLBERT

(13 to 15)

Until I was eleven years of age I had always lived in the country, and my list of acquaintances and my knowledge along every line was exceedingly limited.

In 1884 my father, having gained some political importance, decided to remove his family to a small city near by.

I can't say whether I was pleased or displeased at the idea.

I thought that town life would be very interesting, but I shrank from leaving the little farm where I had been so free and happy, and the thought of leaving Ella almost broke my heart.

I shall never forget the expression on her face when I told her that I was going away. For a moment her dark eyes sought mine to see if I were not jesting; then they fell to the ground and tears began to gather.

Not another word was spoken. I walked away and left her, for my own eyes were strangely dim.

For two or three days we were both very despondent; but we were children, and after a time the keen edge of our grief was worn away.

As we were to move the following Wednesday, Ella and I were never separated now during the day. We talked of nothing but our love for each other and our separation. Childish tokens of affection were exchanged, with vows of eternal constancy, and many plans were laid for the future.

Monday came and passed, and we stood alone in front of the old country school house, her brothers and mine having started for home as soon as school was dismissed.

I knew I should see her no more, for I could not bear to witness her grief at the final separation, and had decided to stay at home on Tuesday.

I held her hand for a moment, during which it seemed that I was parting from the last hope of salvation from an utterly ruined life.

She begged me to come early the next morning, but I made no reply. The tears were streaming down my cheeks, and turning, I ran away and left her.

It was a year before I saw her again, but during that time there was not a day that I did not think of her and love her.

I was very much disappointed with town life. I had no place to play and I hated the noise and dust of the streets.

Seeing so many handsome men, I was constantly tortured with my unnatural desire, and more frequently resorted to self-abuse as a relief.

My elder brothers were away from home during the day, and my younger brother and I were never congenial; hence my extreme loneliness. I loved my sister devotedly, but being much older than myself, and the only girl, she was always too busy to play with me.

My father spoke of sending me to school, but I did not want to go, and my mother, not being favorably impressed with the city public schools, allowed me to remain at home.

I had but one companion, my sister's little dog, and I loved him as only a nature like mine can love. We were together all day, and at night he slept in my arms.

My visits to the undertakers were as frequent as my mother would permit, and I got many new ideas concerning coffins, funerals, etc. Being older and more skillful at my work, my coffins and hearse were now models of perfection, and my little dog horse did his part of the work with almost human intelligence.

Although I loved him with my whole heart, I was not always kind to him. I did not wish to be unkind, but since this new passion had taken possession of me, my bad temper was by no means improved, and upon the slightest provocation I would punish him severely.

As soon as my anger abated, I was always sorry, and often, with tears flowing freely, I would clasp him in my arms and call him all kinds of endearing names as an atonement for my unkindness.

My conscience smites me even now when I remember how submissively he endured my violent punishment, and how happy and forgiving he was when he found that I loved him still

As the days went by he became part of my life, and I simply worshipped him.

One day in early fall, after we had been in the city almost a year, my little pet and I arose early in the morning and after eating breakfast went out to play. I noticed no change in him whatever, but at noon, when I called him for his dinner, he did not come.

I hastened from room to room calling his name, but could not find him. Going upstairs to my brother's room I found him lying upon the bed. As soon as I spoke to him I knew that something was wrong. Instead of springing to meet me as he had been wont to do, he slowly dragged himself to the edge of the bed, and falling upon the floor had a hard fit.

I rushed from the room screaming at the top of my voice.

My mother and sister met me at the landing and learned as best I could tell them the cause of my grief. My sister sprang up the steps, and clasping her little pet in her arms, sent forth a wail of grief almost equal to my own.

My mother was forced to threaten us with severest punishment before our cries ceased.

Our little patient was placed in a room to himself and given every attention, but he constantly grew worse. One fit followed another in rapid succession, and he soon began to froth at the mouth, showing every sign of hydrophobia.

My mother forbade my entering the room, but I sat down by the door, where I could hear every move, and cried myself sick.

His suffering almost drove me mad. I would sometimes go away and leave him, but I could not stay.

When my father came home that evening, he pronounced it a case of hydrophobia, and it was decided that Tolbert should be killed.

When my mother passed the death sentence my grief knew

no bounds. I knew it was useless to remonstrate, but I could not be silent now. With tears streaming down my face, I begged her not to have him killed, arguing that he could do no harm locked in the room alone.

My mother was a woman of sound judgment and never allowed her feelings to influence her against what she thought to be right, so she told me that it was useless to argue the point.

For the first time in my life I, too, was obstinate.

Springing to my feet and dashing the tears from my eyes, I said: "No, I will not argue the point. He shall not be killed, and that settles it."

My face must have indicated my feelings.

My father and mother exchanged glances, and I was sent from the room. I expected to be punished severely, but I didn't care. A great point was at stake, to gain which I would at that moment have sacrificed my life.

Hastening to the window of the sick room, I found my little pet lying down but breathing very hard. I called his name, but he did not heed me, and sinking down under the great weight of grief I again burst into tears.

I was called in shortly and sent to bed, but not until my mother promised me he should not be killed.

I lay there and silently wept, and prayed for his recovery till I fell asleep.

When I awoke in the morning my first thoughts were of Tolbert. I longed, yet feared, to know the truth.

Hastening to his room I found him standing upon his feet and breathing naturally. When I called his name he looked up at the window and wagged his tail. Tears of joy sprang to my eyes, and I ran to my mother and sister to tell them that Tolbert would live.

After breakfast I was allowed to enter his room. He seemed much better, and I was sure he was almost well. I offered him food, but he refused to eat. Thinking, perhaps, he was thirsty, I brought him a pan of water. He drank eagerly for several minutes.

I was delighted, for I was sure that this would give him an appetite.

When he had finished he turned to walk away. He had not gone ten steps when he fell flat upon the floor.

He never breathed again.

My little dog was dead.

The late hope of his recovery served but to augment the sorrow of his sudden death. I fell down by his side and wept till my mother came and took me away.

I don't think there was a dry eye in the house; even my mother wept when she tried to console me.

I ran away and hid myself that I might give full vent to my first great sorrow. I wept till the source of my tears was dried up, and then stole back to gaze once more upon the body of my little companion.

A flood of memories swept o'er me now that almost crushed me into the earth. I remembered what he had been to me, and, saddest of all, I remembered how often I had been unkind to him. Remorse was added to sorrow, and it seemed that I could not stand it.

I knew that he must be buried, but I felt that I could not make the coffin or dig the grave. One of my brothers, seeming to understand my feelings, performed this office for me, and the next day my little pet was buried.

To the other members of the family it was only the loss of a much-loved pet, while to me it was something more. He was the only friend I had who loved me as my nature demanded.

For several days I ate almost nothing and was constantly in tears. I would steal off to the garden alone, and crouching down behind an apple tree, would weep for hours at a time.

Of all sorrows, the greatest is the sorrow of remorse.

If I could only have forgotten my unkindness to him, or if he had shown some little resentment when I misused him, my grief would not have been half so intense or lasting. If I had only had some one to love me in his stead, to talk to me, to console me, I could have borne it better, but no one understood me.

Weeks passed, and time at last taught my heart submission.

While I still loved my funerals and coffins, I never indulged in them much as play after the death of little Tolbert.

Having nothing now to amuse me out of doors, I turned my attention and my love to my sister and my dolls. It seemed that I loved her more than ever before, and I was almost constantly seated at her side playing with my dolls, while she was engaged in more useful pursuits.

Soon after the death of Tolbert we moved about two miles from the city to a little farm, and I was started to school in the country. This helped to divert my mind from my grief, which was by no means forgotten.

Soon after school opened I conceived a very strong friendship for a little boy about my own age and in my own class. The feeling was mutual, and soon we were fast friends. There was nothing of a lustful nature in our attachment, but we loved each other dearly and, with my friend at school and my sister at home, I was again almost happy, when another cloud appeared.

One Saturday afternoon, when sister and I were out for a walk, she told me that she was going to be married soon to a young man who lived far away in another town. I at once began to cry, but to console me she told me that I should go and live with her, and that we would always be happy together.

So beautifully did she portray our future happiness that before the walk was over I was almost glad she was going away.

Spring came, and with it my sister's marriage. I did not go with her at first, as I was in school, but was to join her as soon as school closed. Of course, I missed her sadly, but all of my days and many of my nights being spent with my little schoolmate, I got along fairly well.

As our summer vacation was a very short one, it was decided that I should not visit my sister till after the fall term of school closed. I was greatly disappointed at first, but I had become accustomed to her absence, and being allowed to visit my little friend when I wished, I passed the time very pleasantly.

Now that I lived in the country again I was not troubled so much with lustful desires for my own sex, not seeing so many handsome men. Sometimes the desire would sweep over me like a tempest, and my only relief came in the usual way, but these times were comparatively infrequent.

Before the fall term of school closed my father bought a farm adjoining that of Ella's father, and we at once moved to it.

I was delighted at being near Ella again, but grieved at leaving my new friend and classmate. We spent several days together before I went away, and the morning before I left we bade each other an affectionate farewell, and I never saw him again.

We wrote regularly for several months, but one day in early spring the black mantle of Death wrapped its sable folds about him and all was over.

CHAPTER V

My Conversion

(15 to 17)

After my sister's marriage most of my time was spent indoors.

I still loved my dolls and coffins and played with them at times, but being now past fifteen years of age I began to be ashamed of such amusement. I sewed more than ever, but it was usually upon some useful garment or piece of embroidery, at which I was now taking lessons.

Being small for my age, effeminate in every way, and well known to everyone in the neighborhood, I, as far as I know, escaped any very serious comment. In fact it was considered quite proper for me to stay in the house and assist my mother after my sister's marriage. In this way I escaped all forms of manual labor and every chance of physical development.

As I grew older my passion for men grew stronger, but I had never had a chance to give it expression.

In the spring of '86 something occurred which served to place a check upon this evil inclination, without which I don't know where I should have drifted.

On the first day of April one of the field hands, who had been sent to the village near by, returned bringing me a letter. I did not recognize the writing, but the postmark was that of my little class-mate, with whom I was corresponding.

Supposing it to be an April Fool, I broke the seal with a smile and read as follows: "I write to tell you that George will never write to you again, for he is dead."

With this sentence there came a voice which whispered:

"Be a Christian. Prepare for death."

Of course, I was shocked at the news of his death, but this warning seemed to take the place of grief, and for several days I thought of nothing else. After a week had passed, the impression became less urgent and was finally almost forgotten.

Shortly after this I went for a long visit to my sister, who lived several miles away.

One morning when I first awoke the impression came over me again with doubled force. I felt that I was the greatest sinner living, and that unless I became a Christian at once I should be lost forever.

I was perfectly miserable.

I went out into the woods and wept and prayed for hours, but found no comfort.

I was called to dinner, but I could not eat. In the afternoon I went back to the woods and continued my prayers till nearly four o'clock, with the same result.

Not knowing what else to do, I made up my mind never to do wrong again and to pray every day for pardon.

With this new resolve, I returned to the house, where I found awaiting me an invitation to attend a children's party that evening.

I knew that it was wrong to go, but promising myself that I would neither play nor dance, I decided to attend.

The result may be imagined. I joined in with the rest and danced and romped till almost midnight.

The next day I was miserable again, for I felt that I had done wrong, but in a few days the feeling wore off and did not trouble me again till several months later, when I was attending a protracted meeting in the country.

According to custom, after a long sermon a song was sung and the anxious were invited to the altar for prayer.

I felt that I was a great sinner and longed to be a Christian, but I did not have the courage to go to the altar.

When the song ended and no one had gone forth for prayer, an old man with white hair arose, trembling with emotion, and said, as the tears ran down his cheeks: "If they won't go to Heaven with us, we must go by ourselves."

I shall never forget his words.

All was total darkness around me, and before I realized it I was seated at the altar. One of my brothers came and talked to me, but his words brought me no comfort. When the services closed, I was more miserable than ever, and resolved never to go to the altar again.

I spent the afternoon in the woods alone, praying for relief; but finding none, I stole back to the church, and there alone I tried to give my heart to God.

Night came and I could neither eat nor sleep. I went to church, however, but kept my seat. After services I went to my brother's for the night, but dared not close my eyes, lest I should die and be lost.

By morning I was completely exhausted, but I could not give up the struggle.

I resolved to go out into the woods and pray one more time, and if I did not find relief I would promise God never to commit another sin.

I thought this was possible, for I was only a child.

I would also pray every day as long as I lived, and if, in the end I was lost, it would be no fault of mine.

With this resolve I went to the woods to pray.

The long prayer ended and I felt no change.

Raising my eyes and hands toward the Heavens, I made the foregoing vow and started for the house.

I had not gone twenty yards when—Ah! my dear reader, I wish I could make you understand what happened at that moment.

The great burden of sin was rolled gently from my soul. The sun burst forth from the clouds, the birds began to sing, and I was happy—Oh! happy as the angels in Heaven.

In everything I traced the presence of my Redeemer. I raised my eyes to the heavens and beheld his face in the cloudless sky. I saw his smile in the golden sunshine, and heard his voice in the gentle whispering breeze.

I seemed to be borne along by an unseen hand till I reached the house.

I loved everything and everybody alike. The rankest weed and the fairest flower were just the same to me. They both had fallen from the hand of God and were beautiful in their way.

The smile of youth and the wrinkled brow were fair the same, for I saw them now with other eyes than mine.

When I reached the church I longed to tell the congregation of my new-found joy, but timidity held me back.

Dear reader, if you have ever given your heart to God, you know how I felt that day; if not, no words can make you comprehend, so further attempt is vain. Before you can understand the sweet peace of a soul that has leaned upon Christ for repose, "Ye must be born again."

In all things else I may be perverse and unnatural, but of one thing I am sure, "I know that my Redeemer liveth," and that upon this memorable day I trusted him with a simple childlike faith.

For several weeks after my conversion, I led a devoted Christian's life and was perfectly happy. I prayed several times a day for strength to resist every sinful desire, and during that time was never sorely tempted. But finally I began to be careless about my devotions. One sin after another crept back into my life, and before I was aware, I had drifted far away from the sweet influence that had made me so happy.

Since then I have prayed time after time and made solemn vows to God, but I cannot recall that sweet peace that once clung so soothingly about my soul.

After my conversion, my love for my own sex divided itself into two distinct forms, spiritual and animal, that since then have been at constant war with each other. My love, both spiritual and animal, has always been for my own sex.

With the exception of my attachment for Ella, I have never felt one thrill of love or passion for a female, and even my feeling for her was nothing more than a strong friendship.

Most of my friends however are ladies; my feeling for men being love instead of friendship.

My effeminate manner being interesting and congenial, I have but little trouble in making friends of the ladies, while with men it is different. They either love me or do not like me at all; of course more frequently the latter, but not always, as you shall see.

Soon after my religious experience, Ella and I again started to school at the old country school house.

We loved each other still, and our roads being the same, we

had many pleasant chats as we walked along through the green lanes and shady woods.

I loved her just the same, but she was timid and shy and shrank from me when I attempted any manifestations of affection that had characterized our attachment in earlier childhood.

At this time another evil found its way into my life—that of novel reading. I did not study very hard in school, and since I had to a great extent ceased to play with my dolls, I spent all my spare time reading novels.

I did not care for detective or Indian stories, but Bertha Clay's sad, sweet tales of love filled me with keenest delight.

When I should have been taking exercise, I was crouched down somewhere alone, dreaming, smiling and crying by turns over some sentimental love story.

I kept this up for several years and even wrote two or three stories myself.

From the reading of such literature I formed all sorts of incorrect notions of life.

I became disgusted with the matter-of-fact world around me and was always seeking some ideal character like Edna Erle, in "St. Elmo," and Dennis Fleet, in "Barriers Burned Away."

I had read so much flowery language that I shrank with disgust from any coarse or blunt expression. My own language was becoming very flowery and, I am afraid, very ridiculous.

I often became so much absorbed that I did not take time to breathe regularly, and have gone without my meals rather than give up my novel for half an hour.

I was still annoyed with a desire for my own sex, and every handsome or well-developed man I saw filled me with lustful desire. I longed to clasp him in my arms, to kiss his lips; in short, to devour him, but I had never yet had a chance to do so.

The time, however, was drawing nigh.

It happened one night that two or three young men came to my home to spend the night.

My younger brother not being at home, it was decided that one of them should sleep with me. I was delighted, but for some cause, was scared almost to death.

I very timidly undressed and went to bed, and when by

chance he touched me under the covers, I trembled from head to foot.

He was not so timid, for we had not been in bed five minutes, when he turned toward me and boldly placed his hand upon my sexual organ, which was already erected.

Upon this discovery he placed his strong arms around me and drew me up close to him, at the same time placing his cheek against my own.

I could hear my heart beating, and it seemed that the blood would burst from my face.

He then unfastened my clothing and his own and brought his organs and body in close contact with mine.

I was simply wild with passion. All the pent-up desire of years burst forth at that moment.

I threw my arms around him, kissed his lips, face and neck, and would have annihilated him if I could.

The intense animal heat and the friction between our organs soon produced a simultaneous ejaculation, which overstepped my wildest dream of sexual pleasure.

He turned his back to me and was soon fast asleep, while I lay there scared and panting from sheer exhaustion.

The work was done.

That night the ball and chain were clasped about my ankle and I shall drag them to the grave, and maybe beyond.

The next day I was very unhappy. I had been guilty of a most shameful act and my conscience has never been easy since. I made up my mind never to repeat the offense, but the temptation was too great.

My sexual desires, which had always been strong, were now a perfect fever. I flamed with desire for every handsome man I saw.

The young man in question made more frequent visits to our house after this, and we always contrived to sleep together, with the same result.

I always left him to make the first advance, which he was never slow to do, sometimes beginning before we were fairly under cover, yet not too soon for me.

I had a very handsome brother ten years my senior with

whom I fell in love, and for several weeks I burned with desire to see and handle his sexual organs.

One night when his bed-fellow was away from home, I was allowed to sleep with him.

I retired very early and lay there waiting for him.

'Twas after ten o'clock when he came to bed, and the long period of restless anxiety and my extreme lust had entirely overcome me, and when he lay down beside me I lost all control of myself.

I could neither speak nor move.

My muscles jerked spasmodically and I trembled as though I had an ague. I was very much alarmed, but my brother was either asleep or did not discover my condition, and I could not get up or call any one.

I suffered this way for about half an hour when my self-control returned, but I did not go to sleep at all, neither did I touch my brother.

It was perhaps a year before I slept with him again, and upon this occasion I did not lose my self-control, and as soon as he was asleep, I placed my hand upon his parts which were very flaccid and remained so in spite of my touch.

I did all I could to arouse his passions but failed completely.

I was sorely tempted at this moment, but I did not yield, and with this night my new temptation disappeared for many years, and with it every spark of passion for my brother, and I have never had an incestuous inclination since.

Condemn, dear reader, as much as you choose, I shall not complain; but just remember, "He jests at scars who never felt the wound."

Ye giants of moral and physical strength, ye delvers into spiritual and scientific lore, be for one week what I have been for almost twenty years, and *then* deal out condemnation or pity corresponding to results.

CHAPTER VI

HIGH-SCHOOL LIFE

(17 to 19)

When we were seventeen years of age, Ella's father placed her in the village high school, two miles from our home, and I was kept in the country school alone—yes, alone, for Ella was everyone to me.

I wanted to go with her, but for some reason my mother would not permit me, and being still subject to her command, I went another term to the country school.

When my school closed I at once joined Ella who, I discovered, had advanced very rapidly, and left me far behind.

With this knowledge, a new desire swept over me; a desire to equal and, if possible, to excel her in classwork.

Dolls, coffins, novels, everything but unconquerable lust were thrown to the winds, and I believe even that would have been forgotten, in a measure, but for my teacher and one young man in school.

I should have been in the fourth grade, for I had never studied well, but I jumped to the sixth. I took seven difficult studies and worked as but few have ever done before.

I studied almost every moment of my time. I tormented every one at home almost to death for information, and never slept any night before 12 and often not before 1 or 2 o'clock.

I lived with my book in my hand, and had it not been for my long walk to and from school, I believe I should have collapsed for want of proper exercise.

Ella was the brightest pupil in school, and I had a great work to accomplish, but I was backed by the powerful determination of an extremist on every line and I never wavered.

At first I was not even thought of as her intellectual equal, but after a year of such application our names began to be mentioned together.

At the end of another six months she awoke to the fact that her earliest and dearest friend was also her strongest opponent in the race for honor and distinction.

She bent every energy to her work, but she had not begun in time.

I was not and am not to-day her equal intellectually, but I was believed to be—a belief that stung her keenly.

If she excelled in mathematics, I excelled in something else. If she read well, I excelled in penmanship.

One Friday we were told to write a composition to be read in the English class on Monday.

I glanced at Ella. A frown had settled upon her face, but soon it passed away and resolution took its place.

The best production was to win three extra cards of merit, and I felt that I was bound to win. It was to be left to a vote of the class, and I feared no one but Ella, and it was plain she feared no one but me.

Saturday came. With tablet and pencil I climbed up into the hay-loft and wrote as I never dreamed I could.

My theme, of course, was a sad one, and I gave it full expression.

Tears ran down my cheeks as I wrote, and I felt that I must succeed.

Monday morning came and with it the English class.

Ella's face was a study, but I could not read it.

She read last of all the girls, and I of all the boys.

Her turn came first, and she read in a clear, firm voice, during which I suppose I breathed, but I do not remember it.

Her production was excellent from every standpoint, but it was practical common sense, and I had no fears, for I knew the voters would follow their feelings and not their judgment.

My name was called, and I stepped slowly forward and read in a gentle, subdued tone.

I felt the tears starting to my eyes as I proceeded, but I knew that I must not cry, and I forced them back.

When I had finished, all the girls were in tears.

The vote was cast, and I was pronounced unanimous victor.

At rest, congratulations were showered upon me, but I was not quite happy. The expression of disappointment that shone out through Ella's smiles as she congratulated me cut my heart like a knife. I felt that she deserved the honor herself, for her work, from a practical standpoint, was far superior to mine, and even as a literary production it would not have fallen short if considered by competent judges.

After this we were opponents indeed, and we were pretty well matched.

Study as I would, my evil desires forever haunted me.

I was passionately in love with the principal of the school, and longed for a chance to give my feeling sexual expression. He loved me in return with the love that a true teacher feels for a diligent pupil.

We often talked together, but if by chance he touched me in any way, I trembled from head to foot.

One night, when we had met at the school building to practice for the closing entertainment, he came to me after we had finished and insisted upon my spending the remainder of the night with him.

My time had come.

Of course, I accepted his invitation, and we went to his room together.

We retired at once, and after he had gone to sleep, I carelessly threw my arm across his body.

This awoke him, and he called my name.

I did not answer, and thinking I was asleep, he placed his arms around me, and gently hugging me to his breast, he whispered, "God bless this boy."

There was no passion in his voice or embrace. He loved me with the sweet, pure love of a brother and that was all.

I felt that I should like to die with his arms about me, his cheek against my own.

I felt his warm breath on my neck and shoulder, and my passion began to arise.

I longed to know him sexually, but I dared not take the step. He loved me with a love that I could not hazard for the sake of lust.

He was soon asleep, but I did not close my eyes all night.

I was in bed with the one object of my desire, and yet I dared not touch him.

Do you know what this means? If so, you know why I did not sleep.

After hours of perfect torture this weary night finally dragged away, but the long nervous strain had almost killed me.

Ah, my dear reader, not one but scores of such nights with different men, have brought premature wrinkles to my brow and gray hairs to my temples.

I had a classmate at this time who was about my own age and with whom I was in love.

He liked me very much, and I could see that he was of an amorous nature.

I went to his home with him one night and found him all that I could wish. He was affectionate and amorous in the extreme, and I was the same—what more was needed?

We were close friends and even roommates for several years after this, but we soon became tired of each other in a sexual way, and such relations almost entirely ceased.

In the neighborhood, there was a certain violinist for whom I had always felt the strongest passion.

He was very tall, handsome and well-proportioned and weighed about 180 pounds.

He was a fine musician and much liked by all who knew him.

He and my elder brothers were quite intimate and he often came to my house, but he never slept with me, and many a night after he had retired with my brother have I lain awake for hours, almost aflame with passion.

At such times no sleep came to my burning eyelids till I had sought relief in the usual way.

I had a married brother who also liked him very much, and often invited him to his home to spend the night.

I began to watch for one of these nights. It soon came and I met him there.

I carried my books along and studied till time to retire.

Of course we slept together, and after he was asleep, I cautiously placed my hand upon his genitals.

An erection followed and he awoke at once.

I did not remove my hand, for I knew he was not displeased.

After a moment had passed, he unfastened his clothes, rolled over against me, hugged me to his breast——let curtain fall.

After this his visits to our home were more frequent, and he always insisted upon sleeping with me, stating that he had conceived a great liking for me, and that, as I was always studying, he could not talk to me till I had retired.

This speech was satisfactory all round, and we kept up our sexual relations for several years till he died of pneumonia.

After a night with him, my whole being seemed to relax and I felt refreshed and would have been happy but for my ever-gnawing conscience.

Such intercourse was perfectly natural to me.

I believed self-abuse to be a far greater sin, and I resolved to quit it entirely.

I desired with all my heart to be pure and good, but this evil passion would not permit me.

I took a solemn oath before God that I would never be guilty of self-pollution again.

To render it more binding, I wrote the vows on paper to which I signed my name.

In the next three years I suffered a hundred deaths. I never once thought of breaking my pledge; and now at night when under the influence of lustful desire, I could do nothing but lie awake and suffer.

This I did, not once but often, from dusk to dawn.

I continued in school with Ella and pursued my studies with increasing zeal till June 1890, when we both graduated with equal honor.

Our teacher had accepted the principalship of a college in a distant town and was to open his school the following fall.

Much to our surprise and delight, she and I were chosen as assistant teachers, yet we were only nineteen years of age.

I felt that I could not fill the place, but my teacher was sure that I could, so it was settled that I should go.

My parents readily gave their consent, and on the appointed day I left my home to face the strangely checkered life before me.

This was the first time I had ever left my home for any great length of time, and of course I knew nothing about the ways of the world beyond the suburbs of the little town in which I was educated.

I was to board in the same house with my teacher whom I loved so fondly, and as home had been such in name only since my sister went away, I had no fears of home sickness.

During the weeks of preparation that preceded my departure, I was very happy indeed.

I had, at one bound, arisen from the position of pupil to that of a "college professor"; and although I have never been called self-important, I think I felt my share of pride at my sudden advancement.

Yes, I was very happy, for often "Fools rush in where angels fear to tread."

Could I have suddenly opened my eyes to the dark future before me, I believe I should have chosen self-destruction instead, but I was closely wrapped in the folds of that strange translucent veil of hope and ambition that admitted the lights and excluded the shadows of the long dark years before me.

CHAPTER VII

My First Great Love

(19 to 22)

On Saturday afternoon, the Principal, Ella and myself, with four more teachers, landed in the town of A., and Monday morning school began.

We opened with over 200 pupils, and all was bustle and confusion.

The afternoon was spent in giving to each of the pupils a list of the books to be purchased.

I was secretary of the board, and Ella my assistant. We sat upon the rostrum in the chapel and prepared the lists.

It was almost four o'clock, and our work was nearly finished.

Only two little boys remained, and the principal addressing the larger, asked him what books he needed.

He began to enumerate: " 'Rithmetic, Speller and Eperlectic Gogerfry."

At this blunder, the little boy beside him glanced up at me and smiled.

Ah, my dear reader, I wish I could make you understand.

With that smile my whole life, my very soul was changed.

A strange feeling swept over me—a feeling so sweet, so elevating, so ennobling, and yet so overpowering that I almost swooned.

With that smile I was changed from student to teacher. A full sense of my responsibility fell upon me like a thunder bolt, and I reeled beneath the weight.

Every lustful feeling and sinful impulse died within me, and I was happy! happy!!

I gazed upon the little face and form before me, and my melted heart found expression in a flood of tears.

Ella asked me why I wept, and I told her I was happy.

Our work was finished, and we started home, but I did not care to talk.

I longed to be alone to dream of the sweet little angel that had stolen so softly into my very soul.

I had seen him but once, but that was sufficient. My whole heart had gone out to him, and for over a year I believe I loved him as no human being was ever loved before,

To have seen his face, I would have turned from the grandest picture that the world of art has ever conceived.

To have heard his voice, I would have sacrificed the sweetest music that ever thrilled a human soul.

From that hour everything was forgotten but duty and love. No task was too difficult, no labor too great if duty beckoned me on.

I was always smiling, always happy, and life was one endless summer dream.

I was with him every day and dreamed of him at night.

I taught all his classes but one, and he always recited well.

As he entered my room for recitation, he would glance at me with that same little smile.

If, at any time, he unexpectedly came into my presence, my heart would give one exultant bound, and often tears of joy would spring to my eyes.

Not wishing to be accused of partiality, I talked with him but little during school hours; but ah, those afternoons we spent together!—to me they were part of "Heaven's best bliss," and I was happy.

When Saturday morning came, we would steal off alone for a long ramble in the woods, and in the afternoon we fished in a stream near by.

I would always throw in my hook to please him, but I gave it no attention.

I would sit for hours with my eyes fixed upon his face as he intently watched the bobbing of his cork in the stream.

I studied every expression as it came and went till I almost knew his very thoughts.

In my mind were mingled sad and joyous musings, but they were always sweet and beautiful.

I imagined my little darling had fallen into the river.

I pictured him struggling with the angry current, his little face pleadingly raised to mine for assistance; then came the risking of my life to save him; the rescue and the joy that followed.

I could feel the little dripping form in my arms, his pallid cheek resting against my own, his arms about my neck.

Tears would spring to my eyes, and I would bow my head in reverence for such a love as this.

One Friday afternoon, he came to me and told me that he was going away with his mother, and would not return before Sunday evening.

My heart sank within me, for I had never imagined two whole days without him.

I said but little, but he must have seen the shade of pain that settled on my face, for he hastened to say that he did not wish to go, but could not avoid it.

The next day was the longest I have ever spent. I slept as late as I could, and even then I thought the forenoon would never pass.

I wandered from place to place, but all was lonely and sad. I missed him everywhere I went, and no one could take his place.

In the afternoon I started out to walk again. I traversed every street in town, and passed his home a dozen times, yet I knew that he was not there.

The long June day at last had dragged away. The sun had reached the brow of the distant hills, and shone like a ball of crimson flame.

Weary of my aimless search, I had ascended a flight of winding stairs that led to a hall above his father's store, and sat on the threshold alone.

I bowed my head to dream of the love that was more than life to me.

I heard a step on the stairs below, but I did not raise my head.

Nearer it drew, and in a moment more a hand as light as the summer breeze was laid upon my knee. I raised my eyes— oh, joy divine! my little love was there.

My soul rose up from earth to heaven, and tears were coursing down my cheeks.

I took his little hand in mine, and the golden sun sank down to rest behind a distant crimson cloud.

The sweetest moment my life has ever known too swiftly passed away—and he was gone.

Oh God, give to each human heart one hour of love like this; assure him that it is a foretaste of eternal happiness, and the knave, the thief will become a Christian!

From the moment I first saw his face my life had been sweet and pure as a mountain rill. No sinful act disturbed my days; no lustful thoughts my nights.

My passions were soothed and composed into a peaceful slumber, and I thought that they were dead.

A handsome man no longer held for me a fascination, and I was free—free from long, wakeful nights of lustful torture, free from fruitless prayers and tears.

For me the long, bright days were golden; the nights were nights of sweetest rest.

My whole being was changed.

I worked very hard in school, but I was never weary.

I lived but for duty and love, and cared for nothing more.

I was expected to go into society, which I sometimes did, but it never gave me pleasure, and whenever I could do so unobserved, I would hide myself in some secluded nook to dream of my little love.

A year stole swiftly by, and all was well.

My reputation as a teacher of the young was made, and I did not know that I was succeeding at all—in fact I had not thought of it.

My love had made me what I was.

At this time another professor was employed in the town, and came to our place to secure board.

He was about twenty-three years of age, handsome, refined, and very interesting.

I fell in love with him at once, but not in a passionate way.

As we were both of an affectionate nature, my love was soon returned, and we spent much time together.

I was very happy with him; in fact, I was always happy then. We kissed each other a dozen times a day without a thought of lust. He never wearied of my affection, and always returned it heartily.

I did not love him half as well as I loved my little boy, but it was very sweet to be with him. We did not room together, and when one of us was out at night the other would always sit up and wait for his return and the good-night kiss.

He would often bring his guitar to my room and sing to me sweet, sad songs of love. When weary of singing we would lie down together upon my bed and fall asleep in each other's arms.

So three months passed by and I was happy still.

I had almost forgotten the dark, sinful past, and had never dreamed of its return; but, alas! my house was built upon the sand.

One Monday morning I went to school light-hearted and gay as usual, for I knew I should soon see my little love again.

I met him with the same affectionate smile and greeting, but he only turned away and did not speak to me.

Oh! that awful throb of pain in my heart! I can feel it now.

He came to his recitations as usual, but did not look at me at all when he could avoid it.

I did not question him, for I thought it was a fit of childish pouting and would soon wear off; but I was wrong.

A whole week passed during which he had not spoken to me.

In the afternoon, when I passed his home on my way to the woods alone, he would hide himself to prevent my addressing him.

I could stand it no longer, for I was almost mad.

One day at noon I called him into my room, determined to know the truth.

He did not want to come, but he dared not disobey me, so he slowly and angrily complied.

I placed my hand upon his shoulder, and asked him what I had done to anger or wound him.

He almost threw my hand aside, and answered: "Nothing."

With this he hurriedly left the room and I—no, I will not try to tell you.

Just remember how I loved him, what he had saved me from, and how happy I had been.

No words can paint the black despair that fell upon me when he was gone.

I did not weep—I merely gasped once and sank into the nearest seat.

For several days I was more dead than live, and yet I must labor on in the school.

The lodestar of life had ceased to shine, and all was over.

I loved him more than ever, but he—ah me!

My love became a perfect frenzy.

I longed, prayed but for one more smile and with it instant death.

I worshipped everything that he had touched or even seen.

I watched him all the time when I could do so unobserved, and if he cut a stick with his knife, I gathered up the shavings and kept them because the exertion of his little arm had made them.

One day, after I had seen him trimming his nails, I went to the spot and, finding some of the fragments, I carefully preserved them and have them still.

I found him in the barber shop one day, and after he was gone, I at once had my own hair trimmed and in this way managed to secure a few of his little locks.

I longed for something that he had worn, and I boldly asked his sister to give me a pair of his trousers, which she did.

I disliked to do this, but I knew that I could trust her, for (pardon me) she was in love with me at the time.

This little gift was a great source of comfort to me now, and night after night, when I had retired, I would hug the little garment to my heaving bosom and weep and pray till I fell asleep.

As soon as I had lost his love, I was again besieged by my old passion for men, and it was stronger than ever—so strong that I could scarcely keep from laying hold of strangers on the street.

I struggled to be pure and good, and day after day would fall down on my knees and, in my agony of grief and despair, beg God to help me; to give me strength; to save me from the awful gulf that yawned to receive me.

My tears were vain; my prayers unanswered; my destiny *ruin*.

My love for the new professor was no longer pure, but a burning passion instead.

I soon managed to sleep with him and allowed him to discover that my hitherto sweet, pure love had suddenly grown into a wicked passion.

Although he never referred to the change, and was as kind and sweet as usual, I instinctively felt that he had lost respect for me, and we began to drift apart.

Finally we separated entirely, and I have never seen him again.

Two months passed by, and my little love despised me still.

I did all I could to learn the cause, but failed. His sister knew nothing, and he refused to answer her questions.

I was now a slave to my unnatural passions; my heart was broken, my conscience torn and bleeding, and my life ruined.

School was closing and I resolved to leave the town forever.

I will not speak of the anguish of those last few days and the long, weary months that followed.

But oh, that last look at his little face!

I gave my place to some one else, and went back to the country alone, but I was never the same again.

In eighteen months I had sipped the nectar of heavenly bliss and drank the drugs of keenest pain.

How could I be the same?

Do not sympathize with me, dear reader; I neither need nor wish it now.

Accept these lines in the spirit they are written.

Arouse yourself to action and seek to save some other soul from the anguish I endured.

CHAPTER VIII

IN THE TOMB

(22 to 24)

When I had left A. and the little boy I loved so fondly, I went home to my parents for a few weeks, but I could not bear the dull farm life now, so I went away back into the country and began a little subscription school of fourteen pupils.

I scarcely made a living here, but I did not care, for no amount of money above that necessary for food and clothes could have added to my happiness.

Here I saw but few handsome men, and during the five months that followed, I think I slept, or rather lay awake, with only two.

I boarded in a very nice family, and there I met one of the best friends I have ever had.

She was the third daughter of the family and about 25 years of age. She was very intelligent, interesting and kind, and if it had not been for her, my stay would have been very gloomy indeed.

She knew some sorrow was eating my life away, but she never questioned me; yet she never tired in her efforts to make me happy.

She was a true Christian and knew a Christian's duty.

She would sit for hours talking or reading to me, and her words were my only source of comfort.

Her influence had a tendency to check my evil impulses, but I was still haunted by this torturing desire for men.

I was trying hard to be a Christian, and my prayers for relief were almost constant—yet none came.

Five months passed away and school had closed.

For my fall work, I had accepted a position as teacher with a friend of mine far back in the barrens among people that were scarcely civilized. I did not care for this, for I loved my friend very much and knew that he loved me.

I had never broken my vow, and for several months had not given expression to my sexual desires.

When I saw a handsome man now, my desire became a perfect madness, and I was unfit for work of any kind.

I wept, prayed and struggled more than ever, but found no rest.

A fearful storm was gathering furiously, but I had not even seen the cloud.

It came—it burst forth and swept me into ruin.

I had gone to a town near by to attend the Teachers' Institute preparatory to the fall term of school.

I met many handsome men, and my long abstinence served only to intensify my desire.

My old friend and teacher was there, and the sight of his face and the touch of his hand nearly crazed me.

He seemed very glad to see me, but was worried to find me looking so pale and thin.

He at once arranged for us to spend the following night together at the hotel.

Try to imagine my feverish delight, my lust, and the intense anxiety of that almost endless day.

I tried to attend to my work, but I could not do it.

I thought of nothing but the coming night, and my whole being throbbed with lustful desire.

Night came at last.

After supper, we talked for several hours and then went to our room. I trembled so that I could hardly ascend the stairs.

Two beds were in the room, at the sight of which Passion frowned in anger, and Conscience sweetly smiled.

I feared, yet hoped that he would wish to sleep alone. This he did and we retired in separate beds. I watched him undress and my longing for him knew no bounds.

The anxiety of the day, my present disappointment, and my violent lustful desire were almost killing me.

It was a very warm July night. The moon shone brightly, and the room was as light as day.

His bed was very close to mine, and there he lay, stretched at full length upon his back without a covering over him.

He soon slept soundly, while I tossed to and fro, half frantic with burning passion.

My organs were erected and distended to the last tension.

Terrible pains were in my head, side and testicles, and thus I lay the whole night through.

What could I do?

I could not leave the room, for I had no place to go. My vow forbade my relieving myself, and I dared not touch the object of my desire.

I shall never forget that awful struggle between lust, loyalty and reason.

I was tempted to relieve myself, but Loyalty whispered "No."

Driven on by lust, I arose to a sitting posture, and, putting out my hand, I leaned forward till I almost touched my sleeping Adonis, when Reason dashed me back.

I did all I could to divert my mind.

I wept, I prayed, I struggled without avail.

I tried to imagine my best friend and even my mother lying dead before me, but I could not be calm and serious now.

Morning came at last.

My friend arose and dressed himself.

His own organs were erected, and he made no attempt to conceal them, for he thought I had not awakened.

This was "the last straw."

When he had gone down down stairs, I sprang from my bed and rushed about the room like a maddened brute.

The hot blood tingled in my veins from head to foot, and I hardly knew what I did.

A moment passed—my vow was broken, and I lay panting and exhausted across the bed.

My whole being relaxed, and for a time I thought of nothing.

Suddenly my crime in all its blackness rose up before me, the facing of which was worse than death.

I had broken a solemn vow to God, and I felt that I could never be forgiven.

Self-confidence, self-respect and honor had all vanished in

a moment, and I felt lower than the meanest dog that prowls the streets at night.

I tried to pray, but I had insulted the God of whom I sought forgiveness.

I arose and dressed myself.

I was almost compelled to attend the Institute, which I did in the morning, but in the afternoon I could not return.

I wandered about for several hours, praying for forgiveness and strength to renew my vows.

Late in the afternoon I found myself at the gate of the city burial grounds.

I entered, hoping that the sanctity of the place would tend to solemnize the vows I was determined to renew.

I wandered on for some time in search of a suitable spot to perform these sacred rites.

At last I found an open tomb, and I paused before the entrance.

The bodies had lately been removed, and the walls were falling to decay, but I entered without a tremor of fear.

I went to the extreme back, and falling down upon the cold hard floor, I prayed as I had never prayed before.

I begged God to forgive me for the dark crime I had committed, and to give me strength to renew and keep my vows.

My long prayer ended; my pledge was renewed, and I crept from this solemn abode of death, back into the busy, bustling world of smiles and tears.

I was not happy.

Self-confidence was gone, and I feared that sooner or later I should fall again.

In a week or so my friend and I began our school. We loved each other dearly, and, as we roomed together, sexual relations soon began.

Besides my friend, there was only one man in the community whom I could love in a passionate way.

He was a physician, middle-aged, very handsome and very intelligent.

We spent much time together, and he was never happier

than when tickling, pinching, boxing and tormenting me in every way.

In this way my passions were constantly aroused, and, not daring to betray myself to him, I indulged them more freely with my friend and room-mate.

My conscience was never at rest now. My desire to be good was stronger and my will weaker than ever before.

Seeking to atone for my wicked life by a strict performance of duty, I worked every day in school till I was almost exhausted.

With my wounded conscience, extreme sexual indulgence and overwork, my health began to fail. I declined rapidly, till I weighed but 106 pounds.

I ate ravenously, but I scarcely slept at all, and every morning my clothes and bed were dripping wet with perspiration.

I felt no decided pain, but a heavy weight had settled between my eyes, and I was languid and drowsy all the time.

Everyone thought I should die soon, but no such hope came to me.

At the end of three months I gave up my work and went back to my home in the country.

I was idle for some time and soon regained some of my flesh, but my conscience and evil lusts haunted me just the same.

Two more years of unremitting toil, prayers, tears and remorse passed by, during which my vow again was broken.

During this time I had taught near my father's home, and my relations with the violinist were again renewed.

Our passion for each other had grown much stronger after our long separation, and upon two occasions we resorted to more extreme means of gratification.

In our calmer moments we sadly regretted our act, and it was never repeated.

As a means of diversion, I decided to go again into society. I began to pay special attention to my dress, which hitherto I had sadly neglected, and for a time I was always to be found in circles of social pleasure.

This forced me to flatter and make love to the ladies when my eyes and heart were fixed upon some handsome man, and I shrank from it all with great disgust.

I soon gave it up and was seen no more except at church, and then I was always alone.

I remember one time that there was a minister from a distance, and a stranger to us all, conducting a meeting in our little village.

He was handsome as a picture and very eloquent and interesting, and I was deeply in love with him in a passionate way.

My conscience smote me keenly, but my passions urged me on, and I went to church almost every night. I missed one service, however, but resolved to go the next night and take him home with me.

After church, when I expressed my wishes to have him spend the night with me, he took my hand in his and pressed it very gently.

Looking straight into my eyes he said in almost a whisper: "Why were you not here last night?"

My eyes fell to the floor.

We understood each other perfectly and, breaking another engagement, he spent the night with me.

After we had retired and I was convinced by his poor attempt at snoring that he was *not* asleep, I gently placed my arm around his great manly form.

This was enough.

He turned toward me, placed his arms around my neck, pressed his lips against my own and—forgot to snore.

For once I had found my match.

We slept but little more, and the next morning when my brother asked him how he had rested, he glanced at me and said: "I never spent a more pleasant night."

He went away soon, and I have never seen him again, but I have thought of him more than once.

I was now twenty-four years old, and as I grew older, my life grew darker and more miserable.

My vow had been broken again, and I could not renew it, yet I longed more than ever to be pure and good.

I had no bad habits and had never dissipated along any but sexual lines.

A great weight had settled again upon my brow, and I could not sleep.

My conscience was simply eating my life away.

To the world around me I was forced to smile and appear happy, and my whole life was a living lie.

I was never very sick, but I was growing weaker all the time.

My old teacher had moved back near my home, and I loved him more than ever.

He was married now and father of a beautiful little boy. His whole life seemed centered in his wife and child, but on the 8th of January, 1895, his baby became very ill.

Everything was done to relieve him, but without avail, and the next day he died.

I knew that his father's heart was broken, and I resolved to try to comfort him.

I called at his home that evening, but when he saw me, he covered his face with his hands, and violent sobs shook his manly frame.

My own eyes were filled with tears, and I turned away and left him to his grief.

I spent the night in his home, and there in the presence of the little dead child, it seemed that my dark and sinful life rose up before me with a blackness hitherto unknown.

All that was noble and humane in my nature exhorted me to a pure and holy life, but I could not trust myself to renew my vows.

The night wore on, and with it my misery increased till I could stand it no longer.

'Twas almost eleven o'clock.

Securing a pencil and paper, I framed a pledge to God that, if I could have kept it, would have eliminated from my life every low and sinful act.

About twelve o'clock the other watchers left the room to have a lunch, and I was left alone with the dead.

I knelt down beside the little sleeper and placed my vows in one of his icy hands; the other I took in my own, and bowing my head above his breast, I poured out my heart to God in earnest prayer.

The clock struck twelve.

I arose, took my vows from the hand of death and began life anew.

O, God, thou knowest that I was sincere; thou knowest that I yearned with my whole heart to be a true, good man—*why* could I not keep this solemn pledge?

Months passed, the vow was broken again, and now I was in utter despair.

My life was so dark and sinful that I prayed to die.

I continued to pray for relief, but I had no further faith.

I went to a physician who was said to be very fine, but he had never heard of a case like mine and stared at me like "Simple Simon."

He gave me something to remove the weight from my forehead, but it removed the weight from my pocket instead, and I was worse than ever.

Dear reader, open your eyes to these dreadful facts.

Dream no longer that they are mythical tales that have drifted from Grecian shores.

Such sufferers are all around you.

You worship with them in church; you meet with them at your lodges and clubs; you talk to them on the streets.

Learn to know them; do not spurn them; seek to save them, for they have souls that feel and suffer.

CHAPTER IX

"MY BOY"

(24 to 26)

In the spring of '95, my old teacher again took charge of the school near my home where Ella and I were graduated.

He employed a very fine linguist to assist him, and as I had, at this time, taken only a high school course I decided to enter school and take a course in the languages and mathematics.

I was in no condition for mental work of any kind, but I gave this no thought.

I took up Latin, Greek, French, one branch of Mathematics, and Instrumental Music.

Ella was married now, and I had no especial competitor, yet I plunged into the work determined to drown my sorrow, and to lead my class or kill myself with hard work.

I never retired till after 12 o'clock, and studied every lesson till I could almost recite it from memory.

My progress, though forced and unnatural, was at the same time simply marvelous to my teachers and class-mates.

An unnatural mind was doing a work the natural could not comprehend.

I cared but little for the first honors that always appeared on my monthly report, but still I labored on.

My lust did not trouble me much, for I did not give it time.

With overwork, the weight on my head grew worse, and some days I was hardly sane.

A young man, several years younger than myself, was attending school, and we were best of friends. I loved him very much, but there was but little passion in my love.

He studied very hard and we were constantly together.

His early education had been neglected, and I never wearied

of assisting him with his studies, which he fully repaid with gratitude and love.

Being very wealthy, he often tried to repay me with handsome gifts, which I always refused, arguing that I would rather have his love, for that I could fully return.

We spent many nights together, but no sexual relations ever existed between us.

The first few nights we spent together, I had to relieve myself before I could sleep; but this feeling soon left me, and I thought of him only in a sweet, pure way.

I have always had a great desire to kiss him, but have never done so.

I carefully guarded my dark secret, and as long as he has known me, I don't think he has ever guessed my feelings for my own sex.

I have known him over six years, and I have never found him guilty of a low, unmanly act of any kind.

In every sense of the term, he is a *man*.

A year and a half of feverish toil passed by, and I left college to begin a school of my own.

It was a country school and made up of a very coarse and ignorant class of people.

I was often told by people in the community, that I would have much trouble in controlling a certain boy who always attended and who had, on several occasions, almost broken up the school.

I began with a full determination to break his stubborn will, reduce him to subjection, or have him removed at once.

What do you suppose I did instead? I fell in love with him.

When I rang the bell, he slowly dragged himself into the house looking very sullen and morose.

My heart went out to him with sympathy and love, and I felt like shedding tears.

I then and there determined to make a man of him if possible, and from that hour I had something to live for.

I allowed him to take his course for several days till I could learn something of his true nature.

He proved to be very disagreeable at times to almost all the pupils, yet they liked him, and I could see that he had a great influence over them.

In one moment he could raise a disturbance, and in the next, quell it if he chose.

I at last decided that his disagreeable nature was the outcome of abuse and unkindness at home.

I had learned that his father was a drunkard and his mother worse, "A contentious and quarrelsome woman," and I was sorry for him.

He was sixteen years of age and would have learned very well, but he gave no time whatever to his books.

At first when I spoke to him, he answered me very shortly; but a week had passed now and, as I had always been kind to him, I could see that he was beginning to like me.

One evening after school was dismissed, I asked him to remain a while.

His first words were: "Why, what have I done?"

I smilingly told him that I wished to talk to him on business, and he remained.

I began by telling him that I had noticed the influence he had over the other pupils, and as he was one of my largest boys, I wanted him to help me control the school; that often at noon I would be busy and could not watch the play-ground, and I wished him to see that no trouble of any kind arose.

I also asked him not to speak of our talk to any of his playmates, as they would not understand it.

I could see that he was greatly pleased.

He promised to do as I asked, and from that day I never had any trouble in controlling him and my school. Yet, he would not study at all.

One afternoon, several weeks later, I determined to take another bold step, and asked him to meet me at the school room the next morning at seven o'clock.

He came and, seating myself beside him and placing my hand upon his knee, I began.

I told him how I appreciated what he was doing for me, how much I thought of him, and how anxious I was to have him do well in school.

I then asked him if he could not turn his attention to his books, leave off all his bad habits, and be a man.

He did not answer for some time, but sat buried in deep thought.

Then he said, "Mr. H., you know who I am; you know what kind of a man my father is and what every one thinks of me. It is of no use for *me* to try to be anything."

Tears sprang to my eyes, but I suppressed them, and after reasoning with him for some time and promising to assist him in every way I could, I asked him again if he would not do as I wished.

He refused to promise me, and I admired him all the more, for I knew something of broken vows.

I then asked him to turn his attention to his books, just for one week and see how he liked the work.

This he readily consented to do, and that very day he began.

The change was wonderful, and at the end of the week, he had no wish to turn again to his idle ways.

He bent all his energy to the work with marked success.

He was a natural penman and soon surpassed me in that capacity.

I was delighted and loved him more and more, and he soon became the one object for which I lived.

My love for him was of a sweet spiritual kind, and my passions for a time were almost forgotten.

I rarely ever indulged them now, and my conscience being clear, the pressure on my forehead was not so great.

Oh! if this sweet, pure, spiritual love, such as I felt for him, would ever hover about my soul I could easily be a man—but—no—it cannot be.

He seemed, as the weeks went by, to take a new view of life. He not only mastered his text-books but sought information and advancement from every source.

One day at noon, he came to me and told me that he wished I would kindly tell him of all his faults as they appeared to me, that he might correct them, saying at the same time, that no matter what they were, he would not be offended.

I agreed to do so, and a few days later I ventured to suggest that he gave more attention to his teeth, hair and nails.

The work began at once.

Soon after this, he missed one Friday from school. I was very grieved and worried, but the next Monday all was explained.

He had been to the city and his teeth had been polished till they shone like pearl; a broken one in front had been crowned and another neatly filled.

His nails were in perfect order, and his hair had been trimmed nicely, and was combed with the utmost care.

I was both amused and pleased at the change, and after that, never hesitated to tell him of his faults.

As the days went by, his whole nature seemed to change. He was becoming sweet and gentle in his manner, and I loved him more than ever.

My love was returned, and we spent much time together.

I went to his house one afternoon to spend the night.

I found it a cheerless abode for one who wished to be a man, but this only increased my love and admiration.

We talked till very late and then retired together.

We lay perfectly still for some time when a strange feeling stole softly over me.

I loved him more than ever before, but there was no passion in my love.

I don't know how I felt.

I was certainly not asleep, yet my senses were dazed as though I were dozing.

My whole being seemed to dissolve into a kind of vaporous film that wrapped itself about my friend beside me.

Not a word was spoken.

We lay for a moment more, when suddenly he turned toward me, and placing his hand upon my arm, said in a tremulous voice: "Mr. H., will you excuse me for what I am going to do?"

I assured him that I would, and placing his arms around my neck, he kissed my lips and face a dozen times.

With his arm still about me, he drew up very close to my side and whispered: "Please forgive me. I love you more than anyone in the world, and I could not help it."

I merely said, "That's all right," and soon we were both fast asleep.

We slept together several times after this, but the act was never repeated or referred to by either of us.

As to the cause of his proceedings I have no solution to offer; I leave that to wiser heads than mine. I merely know that it occurred.

Another month passed by, and school was to close in three more weeks with a public concert on Friday night.

"My boy," as I used to call him, was to speak, and I had drilled him with greatest care.

Two or three nights every week, he came a distance of three miles to my home, and I taught him to speak till I was sure he could do it well.

One day, a week before the concert, he came to me with a very sad face (and I thought, a very sweet and beautiful one) and said that he could not speak at the close of school.

I asked him why.

He did not wish to tell me, but I insisted upon knowing, and he said that his brother who was to get him a new suit of clothes would not be at home before the concert, and he could not wear his old ones.

I knew this was true, and I at once made up my mind.

I asked him to accompany me to the city the following Saturday, which he did, and I bought him a nice suit with the understanding that he was to return the money when his brother came home.

I did not doubt his integrity, but was glad of a chance to give it a test, and I had no cause to regret it.

The concert came, and with it my boy's speech.

When he appeared before the audience, he was neatness from head to foot.

People who had known him always, failed to recognize him now.

His face was slightly flushed, but his step was firm and manly.

My heart stood still as he spoke, and I prayed that he might not fail.

His voice was clear and his gestures slow and graceful.

When practicing, he had never done so well, and when the curtain fell, round after round of applause followed.

He reappeared with his violin, and though he had never had a lesson in his life, he had much music in his soul and played two or three old-time melodies with great effect.

When he at last came back behind the scenes, I held him in my arms just for a moment, and glancing up into my face, he felt what I would have said if emotion had not barred my speech.

He only smiled faintly and turned away.

If there was ever a period in my life when I was in any way natural and perfectly happy in the simple performance of duty, it was during this short term of school, but even that must come to an abrupt end, and I must suffer still.

This little concert ended our intimate association; but I am happy to say that he has never returned to follies of his boyhood, but is now a sober, honest and industrious young man, respected and loved by all who know him.

CHAPTER X

FLEEING FROM SELF

(25 to 27)

In the fall of '96, my old teacher resigned the principalship of his school to the linguist and went away.

I was elected first assistant, and I now came as teacher where I had so long been a pupil.

As soon as I was separated from "My boy" in the preceding chapter, my lustful desires returned and with them the pressure on my brow.

When school opened I loved no one in particular, but I soon fell madly in love with one of my pupils, a boy about fifteen years of age.

This was the strangest affection I have ever felt.

I have never been able to decide whether it was love or lust, but I believe it was a mixture of the two.

I felt a deep interest in his welfare and progress in school, and at such times passion was dumb; at other times I yearned to clasp him in my arms and devour him with kisses, and these feelings were accompanied by erections.

I was always afraid of my love for him, and from the beginning felt guilty and unhappy, yet I could not give him up.

My love soon begot a kindred feeling in him for me.

At times he was calm and gentle in his affection, and again his face would flush to a deep crimson, and he seemed restless and uneasy.

Months passed by, and every day we loved each other more, yet we had never given expression to our love.

We met at church one afternoon, and I saw at a glance that his love or passion was unusually strong.

Mine was the same, and after services were over we instinctively lingered around the church door, waiting, one for the other.

When everyone was gone, we sat down upon the steps and talked for several moments.

We were both restless and uneasy, but I hardly knew why. At last he proposed going into the church and sitting down.

This we did, against my better judgment, for somehow I feared, for his sake, to be alone with him.

When we were seated side by side, a love stronger than I had ever felt for him before swept over me.

This was accompanied by that strange, drowsy, vaporous feeling that I had once before felt for "My boy," but now it was strongly colored with lust.

My face burned furiously.

I closed my eyes for a moment, and all was still.

During this moment the same feeling came over him, and throwing his arms around my neck, he kissed me with lips that burned with passion.

This was a warning, and we left the church at once.

After this I was very unhappy, for I feared, and still fear, that I had ruined his life; yet my love for him grew stronger every day, and I could scarcely resist his attempts to make me give it expression.

The weight on my head grew heavier till it was almost pain, and I feared I was losing my mind.

I went to the Insane Asylum and consulted the physicians in charge. I did not tell them my secret at first; but when they told me that unless I got immediate mental relief I would lose my mind, I told them the story of my life and my present love.

They did not understand my case at all, but told me I must give up my school and go away at once.

I asked them if nothing could be done for me, and they said they would search the records for a similar case, and if they could relieve me they would let me know.

I never heard from them, however, and when school closed I resigned and went to B——, a city near by, to seek medical treatment, for I was becoming alarmed.

One Dr. A. was recommended to me as a nerve specialist, and he treated me for some time, without the least effect.

This same physician recommended sexual intercourse with

women as a relief from my trouble, and I made up my mind to try it, though it was the most repulsive remedy ever offered me.

I went to a first-class house of prostitution, and selecting what I called the least repulsive of the lot, we went to her room together.

Well, I have parted from several of my molars, and if sacrificing another would have answered the same purpose—that of satisfying my physician—I would gladly have gone to the dentist's chair instead of to her bed.

I had it understood with her that, "No success, no pay," and after I had failed to sum up sufficient courage for the ordeal before me, she took the matter into her own hands, and so energetically did she [flaunt] her charms (?) before me, that I was completely disgusted.

It seemed that my already flaccid organs would shrivel up and disappear entirely.

I was in a dilemma, and on this especial occasion I was thankful for one feminine gift—a woman's wits in the time of embarrassment.

To relieve myself, I resorted to the following plan:

Closing my eyes so that I could not see the loathsome object beside me, I shut her from my mind and turned my thoughts to a very handsome man, with whom I was madly in love in a passionate way.

Ten minutes passed, and when all was over, she pronounced me a grand success, at the same time modestly (?) insinuating that her charms never failed to "bring em 'round."

Not wishing to wound her vanity, I did not undeceive her, but hastened out into the street with something of the feeling that one ends his first visit to a dissecting room.

This was my first and last sexual experience with a woman, and for several days after, I was almost sick with disgust.

I could see that my physician was greatly amused when I made my report, yet he had too much respect for my feelings to give vent to the mirth that shone in his countenance.

He did not advise me to repeat the experiment, for which I was most thankful.

I then consulted a spiritualist, who offered me much encouragement, but no relief.

As an excuse to my friends at home for my long stay in the city, as much as for the benefit it brought me, I took music and penmanship, and worked very hard.

The city was full of handsome men, and I burned with passion all the time.

I soon found that many others were suffering from a disease similar to my own, and while this knowledge gave me great relief, I was grieved to find the victims so numerous.

One night, while standing upon the sidewalk listening to a public speech, a very handsome and stylishly dressed man about thirty-five years of age, began a conversation with me.

I suspected him of course, for I could see that he labored under some nervous strain, and I decided to let him take his course.

We talked for some time, when he proposed that we go for a walk. I agreed and we walked on down to the river.

When we were in a quiet and dark spot, he placed his arms around my neck and kissed me several times.

Leaning forward, he whispered something in my ear. I had an idea what he meant, but was not sure.

Passion and curiosity tempted me sorely, and I did not repulse him.

Ten minutes passed.

A new experience had been added to my life, and a half slumbering desire awakened in my breast.

One night, several months later, when I was more lustful than usual, I went on the streets actually in search of some one with whom to gratify my maddening passion.

I was passing down a dimly lighted street, when I saw in front of me a man whose form was simply perfect.

I had not seen his face, but I was sure that he must be very handsome.

I quickened my pace, and in the act of passing him I glanced at his face.

One look was enough—too much.

He was all that my passionate soul could desire, and I could not pass him by without a word.

I begged his pardon, then asked him the way to some place that I knew to be in the direction he was going, and he kindly offered to show me the way.

He talked freely, but my own voice was so choked with passion, that I could scarcely answer him.

He soon took on my condition, and before we had gone another block, he had my hand in his and—we were in love.

We turned into a still darker street, for the city was not well lighted, and at that time we did not even have a moon.

He placed his strong arms about me, strained me to his great manly breast and kissed me again and again.

I lay perfectly still against his breast, for I was completely dazed with the sweet blissful feeling his caresses brought to my soul.

He too was aflame with passion, and placing his lips close to my ear, he made a request that I could not grant and I told him so.

He gently put me from him, told me I did not care for him and turned to leave me.

I put out my hand to detain him, and he repeated his request.

I hesitated a moment, and he again placed his arms about me.

I felt my resolution giving way, for oh, how I loved him and how I longed to please him!

Placing his cheek against my own, he whispered: "Will you?"

At this moment reason returned, and springing from his arms, I firmly answered: "No, not if I die," and turning, I hurried away and left him.

I did not look back for some time, and when I did, he was gone, and I knew I had lost him.

I sat down upon a curb completely exhausted by the great strain under which I had been laboring.

I felt at that moment that I would grant any request if I only had him with me again.

I will not describe the rest of that wretched night in my room alone.

Suffice it to say that I met him again, and though men may curse me, I hope God will forgive me if I did *not* send him away.

He was a man sixty years of age, but he possessed a power, a fascination that I *could* not resist.

Even while writing these lines, my hand trembles and my face burns with passion when I remember those wild sweet moments we spent together.

Soon after this, I accidentally met a little man on the streets one night who was affected as I am. We spent the night together, and he seemed to love me very dearly.

My feeling for him was only passion and, after we separated, I gave him but little thought.

He wore a Van Dyke beard at that time, and I did not discover the beauty and sweetness of his face.

When I saw him several weeks later, I did not know him, for he had shaven, but recognizing me, he came at once and spoke to me.

Before I knew who he was, I was deeply in love with him, for without his beard he was beautiful as a dream and fascinating in every way.

We spent that night together, but sweet pure love had completely subdued my passion, and the same feeling soon came over him.

That was a night I shall never forget.

"Passion was dumb and purest love maintained its own dominion."

We lay in each other's arms all night and slept but little.

Our love was so sweet, so gentle, so tender and pure, that even wakefulness was a rest.

We talked of our dark lives, which were very similar, and tears were mingled freely.

We kissed each other a hundred times, and were so happy, the night stole by like a dream.

The next morning he went away, but I was not unhappy, for I knew we should see each other soon.

When he was gone, I fell down upon the bed where we had lain together and thanked God for this sweet pure love.

I began to improve at once.

My evil passion slunk away and hid itself, my conscience was at rest, and the great weight began to leave my forehead.

We corresponded all the time, and he told me in a letter that since our last night together, his passion for men was gone, and he loved no one but me.

I was sure he spoke the truth, for my feelings for him were the same.

He soon came to the city again, and we were so happy that we wept for joy.

He spent three nights with me, and we were so much in love that we almost forgot to take our meals.

I sought no more medical advice, for I did not need it now.

My physician was a man with a soul of love, my physic the love of his gentle soul, and I was well and happy again.

I at once began to take a new interest in life, and learning the merits of the B—— schools, I determined to enter the University there in the fall.

This I did, and all went well for a time.

My beloved friend came often to see me, and life for us both was all joy and sunshine.

I was getting on nicely in school, and the days stole by on golden wings, and the Christmas holidays began. With them came a visit from my friend, and it seemed that we were never so happy before.

He was a Christian, and (smile if you wish) having a sweet musical voice, he would sing sad religious songs to me, which often brought tears to my eyes.

We would sit for hours with our arms about each other and talk of the dark, bitter life from which our love had saved us, and the happy future we were to spend together, but alas! for dreams of earthly joy.

The holidays passed and my friend went away.

From that day to this I have never seen or heard from him again. I wrote to him several times, but received no reply, and my pride, which has always been strong, whispered: "Leave him alone," and I obeyed. I believe he is dead, for he was never very strong physically.

I knew none of his people at all, and as I never signed my

name to my letters to him, there was no possible chance for them to communicate with me in any way.

My love was lost, and now the days crept wearily by.

For a time, grief and anxiety mastered passion, but when hope gave place to despair, I again became an easy prey to lust, and I was miserable.

I burned with desire for my classmates and teachers, and could scarcely hold myself in check. My head began to trouble me again, and I could not sleep at night.

When I retired, it seemed that a weight of a hundred pounds was placed between my eyes, and when I slept at all, my dreams were hideous and terrible.

I remained in the city till April, when school closed, and then went back to my father's home in the country, where I at once began a summer school.

I was again adrift on the wild sea of an abnormal passion, without chart or rudder.

I had a little niece in school whom I had always loved very dearly, and I now turned my whole attention to her educational advancement.

My last disappointment had so discouraged me that I determined to give up all hope of love and recovery, and to make her welfare and happiness the one grand object of my life.

She was fifteen years of age, very beautiful and very intelligent, and I spared neither time nor expense in giving her every possible advantage.

I made a good salary, and had no one else to share it with me.

She advanced very rapidly, and I soon found myself living for her alone.

While the brotherly love I felt for her by no means subdued my passion for men, it to a great extent held me in check, and I was about as happy as I ever hoped to be.

My school continued until about the last of October, when it closed with a concert at night.

The entertainment consisted of music and a drama of my own composition, in which my niece was the heroine, and I the leading man.

The play was very sad, and gave excellent opportunity for good acting.

She took the part of my wife, and in a drunken frenzy I had murdered her.

Then followed my grief beside her coffin, the burial, and lastly, my lunacy behind prison bars.

I had always been a perfect failure as an actor, but I was not acting now.

In these scenes I found an opportunity to pour out before the world all the bitter anguish that had filled my life for almost eighteen years.

I forgot the play, the audience—everything, but the words of the drama, which were written to express the real feelings of my suffering soul.

The audience, I afterwards learned, was deeply moved.

The men were serious and thoughtful, and the women were all in tears.

After the play, a feeling of relief came over me that I cannot describe.

All the sorrow and suffering of my wretched life I had cried out before the world, yet no one knew my secret.

Compliments were showered upon me. I was called an actor and begged to go on the stage, at the absurdity of which I could but smile.

I knew my acting was over. I had told the world of my suffering, but I could not do it again; so I did not take to the stage.

After school closed, it was decided that Violet (my niece) should go for a long visit to an uncle in Texas, and preparations were at once begun.

I had not forgotten how to sew, and with the assistance of an experienced dressmaker, many beautiful gowns were planned and created.

After two weeks of preparation all was ready, and I bade her and affection farewell, and went back to the University, where I was to be graduated in the spring.

I had a letter from her every week. She had reached her uncle's in safety and was very happy.

Her letters were always full of affection and gratitude, and my heart welled up with pride when I thought of the future in store for her.

I was living for her sake, and determined to make her happy.

I slept, I dreamed, and for a time forgot that no hope of *mine* could ever materialize.

Friday came, the day for a letter from Violet.

Instead, there came a telegram, which simply read: "Violet is very low. Can't live."

The next day she died, and Sunday she was buried in a strange land, away from home and hearts that loved her.

I did not weep—no.

My heart simply collapsed, and sinking into a seat, I bowed my head, and the blackness of night closed again around my gloomy life.

> 'Twas ever thus from childhood's hour,
> I've seen my fondest hope decay;
> I never loved a tree or flower,
> But what 'twas first to fade away.

CHAPTER XI

Four Months of Paradise

(27 to 29)

After Violet's death, a kind of stubborn helplessness settled upon me and I did not try to shake it off.

I lost interest in my studies and did not care whether I was graduated or not.

I was tired of "Toil without recompense," and resolved to quit.

I dropped one or two of my studies and gave up every hope of getting my diploma.

What was the use? My life was under the ban, and it seemed that even God refused to help me.

I did not pray now; why should I? My prayers were never answered, and all I had ever held dear had been taken from me, while those who did not pray at all were happy with their loves.

Sometimes in my lonelier hours I would weep, but these times were very rare.

School closed and I went back to my home in the country and taught till October, '99.

When my school ended I became so lonely and discontented that I could not bear an idle life surrounded by old scenes and faces.

There was a man in the town where I was stopping, with whom I was madly in love in a most passionate way, and I had good reasons to believe that the feeling was beginning to be mutual.

Now, since I was idle, my love had become a perfect frenzy and I was miserable all the time.

I could not think of giving expression to my feeling, for I did not trust the object of my desire, and I made up my mind to go away.

I went back up to B——, thinking that if I could get a position, I would not teach any more for a time.

When I reached the city, old scenes brought back old memories and I was more unhappy than I had been at home. I did not know what to do, but it was plain that this was not the place for me.

I walked aimlessly along the streets buried in thought, till I found myself in front of a ticket office. I entered, determined to go somewhere, I did not care where.

New Orleans, Cincinnati and St. Louis came into my mind; but having no choice, I asked the ticket agent what a ticket was worth to—St. Louis, at the same time handing him twenty dollars.

He gave me a ticket and my change, and on November 11, 1899, I landed in this city for the first time.

I spent two weeks in seeing the sights and familiarizing myself with the city in general.

During this time, I had had no sexual dealings with any one, nor had I been very sorely influenced, for the men here have never tempted me as those in the Sunny South.

I did not like St. Louis at all, but made up my mind to spend the winter anyway and began to look about for employment.

I had never done anything but teach, and being a perfect stranger, I did not know how to go about finding work.

I was worn out with mental labor and resolved to pursue it no further.

I was not fitted for manual labor of any sort, and, while walking about the streets wondering what to do, a sign, "Ladies' Tailoring," on a window, caught my attention. I knew that I had not forgotten how to sew, so I boldly entered and asked for work.

It was during the busy season, and help being very scarce, I was taken on one-half day's trial, at the end of which time I was employed.

Soon after this, I met a young man one evening on the corner of Sixth and Olive streets, who was affected as I am and we knew each other at sight. I spent that night at his house and we had a most delightful time. He was gentle, refined and very interesting, and we soon became fast friends.

Our sexual relations ceased at once, and genuine brotherly affection is the only tie that binds us now.

He looks upon his disease as a great misfortune, of course, but has long since learned to bow in submission to the inevitable and now worries but little on its account.

He has been a great source of comfort to me, and I shall always remember his kindness and brotherly advice.

I soon met several men in a social way, but so far had fallen in love with none.

I went to the theatre almost every night, and being very busy during the day, I had but little time to brood over my own condition.

One Sunday evening, while seated in the Columbia Theatre watching the show, a man came in and took the seat beside me.

He was very handsome, and had a sweet, fascinating face, yet I could see that he had been drinking heavily.

He soon began a conversation with me, and I found his voice as sweet and interesting as his face. We continued in conversation, and when the show was over, we were not far from being in love with each other.

He gave me his name and address, and asked me to call and see him. This I did several weeks later. He was not at home, but I was told that he would be there in an hour, and was asked to call again at the end of that time.

It was very cold, and I went into a grocery store near by to wait till the hour passed.

The grocer, turning to me, asked me what I wanted, and I saw his face.

He was not so handsome—no, but in that face was mingled everything that was gentle, noble and good; and I loved him, not in a passionate way, but with a love that subdued the strongest passion.

I turned to leave the store, for I had made up my mind to love no more.

I even walked out upon the steps and closed the door, but I simply could not leave him. I walked boldly back and began to talk to him.

At first he was rather reticent, for, as he afterwards told me, he thought I was making myself a little too much at home.

He is a man who thinks a great deal and says but little, and he saw no reason why he should be communicative to a perfect stranger.

I almost forced him to talk, however, till I, by chance, said something about practical Christianity.

He flashed his eyes upon me—eyes that shone with intelligence and sudden interest—and I knew I had struck the keynote in his soul. I stayed for an hour, and when I left him, we were fast friends.

He gave me a book he had written along the lines of Spiritual Development, which, though far too deep for me, I read with great interest, because *he* had written it.

He wished to know my opinion of the work, and when I had finished it, I wrote him a short note asking him to call at my room the following Sunday afternoon.

He came, and we went out for a long ride on the cars, during which I told him, as best I could, my opinion of his book.

He saw that some great trouble weighed heavily upon my mind, and he wished to relieve me, for in the past he, too, had suffered.

I told him no one could help me, but he would not have it so. He was sure he could teach me to forget my sorrow, and begged me to let him try.

He was so sweet, so gentle, so kind and tender, that my heart went out to him in spite of my resolve to love no more.

When we said good-bye, the light in his eyes and the pressure of his hand told me that his feeling for me was more than a passing interest, and I became alarmed.

The next day I wrote him a long letter, telling him that there was no hope for me—no rescue from the gulf of despair into which I had fallen—and begged him, for my good and his own, to leave me alone.

This served only to intensify his interest, and he came again to see me.

He would not listen to me when I told him my life was over, and when he went away, we loved each other more than ever.

I tried to throw off the spell, but it clung about me still. From the moment I had seen his face my passions were dead.

I went out into the streets and actually tried to regain my feeling for men, but failed.

I longed, yet feared, to yield to the sweets of love, for I was sure that the object of my affection would be taken from me, and I shrank with horror from the awful pain that I knew must follow.

I did not know what to do.

It was plain that if I stayed in St. Louis I should soon love him with every fiber of my affectionate heart, and this I was determined not to do.

I believed that if I went back South, this sweet, spiritual attachment I felt for him, combined with the influence of his weekly letters, would save me from the lustful desire I felt for the man who had caused me to leave my native town.

Reasoning thus, I made up my mind to return to my old position at once, and called to say good-bye to my much-loved friend.

He was grieved to have me go, and asked me to write to him.

This I agreed to do, and when I reached my destination, a correspondence at once began.

I was absent from St. Louis one hundred and twelve days, and in that time I received from him one hundred and seven letters, the shortest of which was five pages and the longest thirty-four.

From the beginning, I was determined not to love him too well; not to allow him to become necessary to my happiness and peace of mind; and above all, not to entertain a hope that he could save me; for I knew that hope was vain and that the black despair which always follows every hope of mine would be worse than death to my sensitive being.

As he did not know the nature of my trouble, and was sure that he could help me, his letters at first were devoted to the presentation of a course of mental discipline by which I might relieve my own mind of its galling burden.

I continued to tell him that my case was hopeless and begged him to give no time or thought to me.

I told him from the first that I was a bad, wicked man, unworthy of his kindness, but he would not believe me. All my arguments only increased his interest, and as the weeks stole by, his letters of advice and instruction gave place to those of affection, and every day we loved each other more.

He begged me to forget my sorrow and try to be happy for his sake if not my own.

I told him that I was perfectly happy at present and loved him with all my heart, but I knew that the sweet dream would fade, and that he would be taken from me.

He implored me to speak no more of fading dreams; he vowed that he would love me as long as he lived, and that after death, his spirit would hover about me and make me happy still.

Many were the tears that stained the page as he strove to assure me that his ardor could never wane, and many were the kisses my lips bestowed upon the stains those tears had made.

Ah, dear reader, his vows were so sacred and solemn, his love such a haven of refuge for my lonely storm-tossed soul, is it a wonder that I again closed my weary eyelids and sank down to rest in a dangerously sweet and blissful slumber?

As the days stole by, my whole heart went out to him and I lived but in the sunshine of his sweet, pure love.

The gloomy sinful past seemed like a story I had read when but half awake, and the future one boundless expanse of happiness and peaceful rest.

My lusts were entirely forgotten, and a handsome man was no more to me than a beautiful picture or a statue of polished stone.

The sweet vaporous feeling of which I have spoken before, clung around me all the time and stupefied my senses to all things inharmonious to my musical soul.

I was sensible of an invisible veil that hung before my eyes and mellowed the harsher outlines of all objects in the range of vision.

My ears were so muffled as to exclude all discordant sounds, and the hitherto shrill whistle of the locomotive now stole upon the sense like the high tremulous note in some sad, sweet song.

The fragrant odors of the flowers were so distilled and purified in the filter of love, that their presence was scarcely known, so light was their silent tread upon the sensitive tablet of consciousness.

It seemed that the great God of Nature had raised to his lips a warning finger and whispered "Hush-h-h" to the whole wide world around me.

Ah-h the peaceful sweetness of those long spring days, the hazy mist on the distant hilltops, and the softened glow of the golden sunshine—why, *why* must I remember them now, when they have faded from my life forever?

Spring advanced with its singing birds and blossoming flowers, but I did not note the lapse of time.

With every mail there came sweet messages from the man I loved, and I was supremely happy the long days through.

My school moved on like the wheels of a clock, and my pupils loved me more than they had ever done before.

I was never angry now, and whenever my patience was sorely tried, I merely glanced at a sweet-pictured face on the wall near by, and all was well again.

When school was out in the afternoon, and the children had gone away, I would lie down in the shade and smile and dream till the muffled sound of the approaching train announced the arrival of a message from my heart's dearest idol.

With a joyous smile, I broke the seal and read again and again each sweet expressive clause.

When evening came, I stole off to my room alone to frame a fitting reply to the loving message that had filled my soul with such unbounded joy.

When the pleasant task was ended, I would yield myself to a slumber as sweet as that of an innocent child, and when morning came, I awoke as happy and free as the birds that sang in the trees around me.

Ah, me, when I seek to convey to another mind an idea of the sweet peace that then filled my own, I find my language frail and powerless.

Week added itself to week, and my school was drawing to a close.

I was going at once to my beloved friend as soon as my work was done, and I counted the moments and even the seconds till I should see his gentle face, and feel his loving arms around me.

Another week passed swiftly by, and school had ended.

I gave up my position, and bidding farewell to friends and loved ones, I hastened to the nearest river port and took passage on a boat bound for the home of the man I loved so fondly.

I will not describe the long voyage that followed.

I will not tell you how late I sat alone upon the deck at night, gazing far away into the mysterious star-lit heavens, or watching the silvery moonbeams that played on the ever-restless waves around me; no—but I *will* tell you that I was happy; yes, happy as the angels in Heaven, and free from guile as the gentle breeze that stirred the folds in the Stars and Stripes above my head.

In this restless, changeful world, spiritual pleasures come like dewdrops to freshen for a time the wilted foliage of our lives, but ere we are aware, they melt away, leaving it to sooner parch 'neath the blistering rays of materialism and pain.

CHAPTER XII

THE LAST DREAM FADES

(29 to 30)

I reached St. Louis June 14, 1900, and found my friend all, and even more, than I had ever imagined a man could be.

I will say for the benefit of those who cannot understand a love like ours, that no sexual relations of any sort ever existed between this man and myself.

He took me in his great manly arms, and with his cheeks against my own, he renewed his vows to love me always.

I took a room very near his home, and for nearly a month I believe I was the happiest being that ever lived in this sinful world.

I was completely bewildered by the sweet spell that had stolen over me, and I never once dreamed that I could ever suffer again.

I was with him every day, and my life was supremely, divinely happy.

Alas, for my blind and slumbering soul, the awakening was near at hand.

On July the third, the dream began to fade.

We had gone down town on the car together, and on our return, he read his paper all the way, leaving me to amuse myself as best I could.

I felt—I *knew*, that his love was leaving me, and I was stunned by the awful knowledge.

I left him with his paper, and went out to Forest Park alone, and it was there that the keenest pain my life has ever known began eating my heart away.

With the prospective loss of his love, the dark, wicked life that I believed had passed forever, rose up before me and almost drove me mad.

Days went by.

He was always kind, but I knew that he had ceased to love me, although for many weeks he did not tell me so.

He never spoke of affection now, and always changed the subject when I referred to it myself.

If I attempted to caress him, he repelled me in a playful kind of way, but it hurt me just the same.

With the loss of his love, old desires crept slowly but steadily over me, and the battle at once began.

I crushed them back with an iron hand, hoping and praying that he would learn to love me again, but hope was vain.

The gulf between us widened till one evening he flatly refused to kiss me, and plainly told me that love for him in this world was over.

I did not offer to touch him again, and he never knew what pain his words had brought to my crushed and bleeding heart.

I went to my room alone; and falling down upon my knees, I begged God to let me die, since he had ceased to love me.

I believed it would kill me to return to the dark, wicked, unnatural life, from which his love for a time had saved me; but "Still comes not death to those who mourn," and even *I* am living yet.

When I was sure I had lost him, my evil desires swept over me and crushed me as they had never done before.

Often, when some dark impulse drove sleep from my weary eyelids, I would arise, dress myself, steal silently to his house and lie down upon his porch, hoping to find relief from simply being near him.

I wept, I prayed, I struggled, but all without avail.

I longed to run away from the city and hide myself, but I could not break away from him, besides I had invested in a new invention all the money I had saved for several years, and, 'tis useless to say, I had lost it all.

I should not have grieved at the financial loss, if I could only have retained his love, but poverty in both heart and purse seemed more than I could bear.

He offered to supply me with means upon which to subsist till I could get employment, but I was too proud to accept them, and there were many days I did not have sufficient food.

I bore my poverty, disappointment and passion as bravely as

I could till the middle of September, when I made up my mind to go away to another part of the city and leave him, hoping that my absence for a time would teach him to love me again.

I got employment in a tailor's shop, and took a small room several miles from his home.

I asked him to write to me, which he agreed to do, but hastened to say that there would be no loving words or exchange of kisses in the letters that passed between us.

This speech so angered me that I could have *crushed* him with my heel, but I merely made some indifferent reply, and he never guessed how deeply his words had stung my pride.

He came once to see me, but wishing to test the love he swore should live forever, I did not return the call.

Weeks passed, but I did not see or hear from him again.

During this time my long pent up lust so clambered for expression that I found no rest day or night.

The weight on my brow was so heavy at times that I hardly knew which way I was going when on the streets.

I withstood as long as I could.

One evening, when it seemed that I burned with desire as I had never done before, I walked out upon the street determined to give my feelings expression if an opportunity could be found.

I had not gone far, when I was attracted by a policeman so handsome and manly that I trembled from head to foot with lustful desire.

I stopped on the corner near him that I might have a better view of his face.

I did not speak to him of course, nor intentionally indicate my desire in any way, but he was wise as he was handsome, and after looking me in the face for a moment, he began talking to me.

He came so close to me that his blue coat touched my arm and thrilled every nerve in my body.

I trembled so that I could scarcely talk, but he was kind enough to help me out.

He told me plainly that he thoroughly understood my case, and was sorry for me.

He held my hand in his for a moment, and looking down into

my very soul with those great brown eyes of his, he whispered, "You need not fear me, my boy; I will never give you any trouble."

With a gentle pressure of my hand, and the faintest, sweetest smile, he turned away and left me.

Almost paralyzed with lust and admiration, I gazed after him till he had turned a corner, and then—well, if I had burned with desire before, how do you suppose I felt when he was gone? I will not try to tell you.

I wandered about the streets till after 11 o'clock, when I accidentally met a very handsome actor, who was playing in one of the theaters that week.

He was affected as I am, and we went to his room together, where I stayed till almost 2 o'clock; but we closed the door, and *you* must neither knock nor enter.

After I had left him, my muscles seemed to relax, and had it not been for my conscience, I should have felt very much relieved.

As I was passing through a very dark and narrow street on my way home, a man sprang from a doorway, and catching me by the arm, gave me two violent blows about the head and face.

In another moment he had gone through all my pockets, and had taken my hat from my head.

I had ten dollars, but he did not get it, as I had followed an old custom of mine before going out late alone, and dropped it in between my leg and clothes.

I tried to find an officer, but failed.

The thief defied me, and made no attempt whatever to escape.

I was not afraid of him, and my life was so dark and stormy, that I almost hoped he would kill me.

He tried on my hat, but it was too small for him both in shape and size.

There is nearly always a ludicrous vein in the most serious matters, and I felt half inclined to smile at the figure he cut in my hat, for he weighed at least 220 pounds, and had a very round and fleshy face.

He took it off and extended it toward me with an oath, saying that he had no use for such a thing as that.

I put out my hand to take it, when he sprang forward and struck me on the right cheek with all his might, then hurried away with hat, small change, knife, and all.

I was two miles from my room, with a broken jaw, and without a hat, and it was during that long, gloomy walk that my conscience did its strongest work.

My face, which had begun to pain me terribly, was swollen to almost double its natural size, and I was sorry he had not killed me.

If ever I hated my unnatural life, it was during that lonely morning walk.

I longed to tear myself loose from the dreadful curse, but I knew that such a wish was vain.

It was sweet, pure love alone that could save me, and no one loved me now.

I thought of my friend, but I knew that he had forgotten me.

Tears of anguish ran down my cheeks when I contrasted my present life with the life I had led when I had his love.

I was almost sure that nothing could relieve me or make me happy now, but I decided to struggle a little longer yet.

I knew that, if I ever yielded to utter despair, the decision would be final, and I had carefully counted the cost of such a step.

I went to see a skilled physician, who was very kind to me. he gave me a prescription without any charges, and told me I must resist these evil impulses.

I knew that resistance would only weaken me, but I did not tell him so.

I took his medicine regularly for about a week, without any perceptible results.

I called to consult a hypnotist, but he was going to leave the city, and could not begin his treatment then.

I had a brother whom I had always especially loved. He was a leading minister in the south, and I felt that his presence might lend me power of resistance, for a time at least.

Accordingly, I wrote to him, begging him to make me a visit, at the same time assuring him that his expenses should be paid.

A month passed by. He did not as much as deign me a postal

card in reply. (He was very busy at the time, however, and I did not tell him why I wished to see him.)

This was *not* the "last straw." There was one more, but *only* one, and I deliberately mapped out my course of action when I should feel its weight, and waited for the time to come.

All this time I had neither seen nor heard from the man I had loved so fondly, and on February 21, 1901, just one year after I had seen him first, I wrote to him asking him to call and see me the following day to say good-bye for the last time.

I did not intend leaving the city, but I knew that he would think this, and that if he even felt a passing friendship for me, he would call to see me.

I was neither hurt nor surprised that he did not come, and when the appointed hour passed, I took a car, and on my way to his home, I adopted the following *final* course of action.

I would never, so long as I lived, make another attempt to find happiness or relief through love. I had done all I could, and my conscience was perfectly clear.

I would be honest, upright, temperate, just and forgiving.

I would never stoop to a low, unmanly act along any but a sexual line, and even there I would resist till resistance gave me pain.

I would carefully avoid notoriety, and never seek to influence or lead astray the inexperienced.

I would write the story of my life, place it in the hands of physicians, and do all I could to arrest the rapid progress of this dreadful disease.

I would not allow my condition to worry me any more, for worry only weakens my power of resistance.

I would cease to hope for recovery, but would continue to submit myself to treatment.

If, by chance, I should find relief, all would be well; and if not, then I would not suffer the agonies of disappointment that have hitherto followed my every attempt to recover.

When I reached his home and asked him why he did not call to see me, he said that he had no one to leave in his store.

I talked with him awhile in an off-hand way, then got on a car and went back to my work a different man.

I will say in justice to him, that I do not blame him for the way he acted.

He is a perfectly natural man, but for a time he was under the spell of my strange affection, and he acted just as he was forced to act.

When the spell left him, he was not to blame that he did not love me still.

I went to see him again soon, and told him the whole story of my ruined life.

He was sorry for me, but his sympathy fell upon a leaden heart.

He is the noblest, purest and most unselfish man I have ever known, and there is nothing he would not do to help me.

He offers remedies of every kind, but his help has come too late, and I often find it a task to give his advice polite attention till he is gone, after which I never allow myself to think of it again.

What is the use?

From such reflections I reap only a harvest of pain without a grain of benefit.

Sometimes a longing for a sweet, pure life steals over me, but with it comes the memory of the long years of fruitless prayers and tears, and I throw it off again.

I do not claim that I have taken the proper step, for I do not know.

'Twas the only one in sight for me, and I am prepared to meet the final results.

For almost twenty years I bravely fought the bitter fight.

Weary and faint from the loss of blood, my hands fall helpless at my sides.

Wounded and scarred, I have yielded up the sword; the field is lost, and all is over.

I am a prisoner for life in the gloomy dungeon of an abnormal passion.

I have tugged at the cruel chains that bind me, till my hands are torn and bleeding, and I can tug no more.

I have slunken back into the darkest corner of my cell, where I fear I shall remain, weary, passive, baffled, till the angel of death shall shove back the ponderous door and set me free, or imprison me forever.

The sweet music of my life is over.

The last sad strains have died away into a mocking echo; but I do believe, that when I have heaved my last sigh and shed my last tear, the great throbbing heart of the Savior will not forget that—

"Frailty, thy name is Human."

CHAPTER XIII

FREAKS, FETICHES AND FANCIES

After the closing of my story proper, I feel that it would not be amiss to mention some of my peculiar inclinations, desires, aversions, etc., of which I have hitherto failed to speak.

As I have said before, my love for my own sex is of two perfectly distinct kinds—spiritual and animal, which dominate each other in turn.

When I love a man in a spiritual way, my lusts are entirely forgotten; but as soon as this love is crossed, my animal nature completely overwhelms me, and I am but little better than a brute.

It is hard to give you a correct idea of the kind of men that attract me most in a spiritual way, as their personal appearance has but little bearing with me.

They may be any size, any type, and almost any age, and if the spiritual gifts are present, I will love them just the same.

They must have a sweet, gentle nature, a kind, forgiving heart, and a great love for the good and beautiful in every form.

They must be as neat personally as their vocation will permit, but no more so.

I do not care what their occupation is. I would love a street sweeper just as quickly as I would a Yale professor, if the sweet soul was there.

Of course, social position, good breeding, and literary training would make him more interesting, if he could possess them and still be natural, but such is seldom the case.

Almost every man whom I have purely loved has been comparatively illiterate and obscure. In such cases a kind of sympathy is present, which adds much sweetness to my affection.

In almost every instance the object of my spiritual attachment would be most repulsive in a sexual way.

I have in mind a little waiter employed at the restaurant

where I take my meals, whom I could love with all my heart.

I should like to fold him gently in my arms and kiss his little spiritual face, but even a thought of sexual relations with him fills me with disgust.

One night, a few weeks ago, when I was more passionate than usual, and could not bear to sit alone in my room, I walked out upon the streets.

I was almost afraid to do so, for at such times I never feel quite safe among so many attractive men.

He had been absent from the restaurant for several days, and I had learned that he was sick.

My heart went out to him in sympathy and love, but on this particular evening I don't think I had thought of him.

I had not gone far, however, till I found myself facing him on the sidewalk. He had been sick, indeed, and was so pale and pitiable-looking that tears of sympathy came into my eyes.

I took his little trembling hand in mine, and gazed for a moment deep down into those sweet soulful eyes of his, and every sexual impulse died within me.

I was so happy that I should like to have stood there forever with his hand in mine, but I felt that strange something stealing over me, and I dared not linger near him.

A few words were exchanged and he went away, but I could not throw off the spell.

I continued to walk the streets for some time, but I neither saw the faces nor heard the voices of the restless multitude around me.

Some time after I had left him, I found myself leaning against the corner of a building, murmuring the lines of a poem which I had never seen nor heard before.

When I had finished, several people were gazing at me curiously, and I walked away.

Long after I had gone to my room, the lines continued to ring in my ears, and I could not sleep. At 2 o'clock I arose, wrote them on paper, and here they are:

> Ye poets, who sing of the moon's pale light,
>> And the light of the sunny skies,

Sing ye to me of the heavenly light
   That shines in *his* sweet, sad eyes.

The moon's soft glow will fade away
   As soon as the night is done;
And that of the skies no longer stay
   Than a cloud obscures the sun.

But the light in *his* soulful eyes will shine
   Through sun and cloud the same,
And fill this lowly heart of mine
   With a joy unknown to fame.

But ah! too well I know that Fate
   Will turn those eyes from me,
And howl in mocking tones, "Too late;
   There is no love for thee."

With this stanza, a feeling of despair took the place of love, and I could write no more, though I tried for over an hour.

I have several times since endeavored to add a few more lines that the ending might not be so abrupt, but as I am by no means a poet, every attempt has failed.

Often one glance at his strangely fascinating face, soothes and composes my passions and places me beyond the reach of the strongest temptation.

Even last night after wandering about the streets for some time in a state of feverish desire, I went and stood for nearly an hour upon the sidewalk opposite to his room. At the sight of his face half hidden by a lace curtain that hung before his window, my evil desire vanished in an instant, and a love, sweet and restful, filled my soul with an almost heavenly joy.

The clock struck eleven.

His window shade was lowered, and I turned away and left him.

I went straight to my room, where I slept the whole night through without another thought or dream of passion.

It is still harder to give you any definite idea of the kind of men that attract me in a passionate way, for I do not understand myself along these lines.

It greatly depends upon the mood I am in. Sometimes it is one style and again another entirely different, but as a rule two types of men attract me most.

They are either very large or smaller than the average, but I never care for very slender men.

The nature of my feeling for the large and the small man is entirely different.

With the large man I like to be just as rough in my affection as he will permit. I enjoy slapping, pinching and abusing him in every way just so long as I don't cause him any very great pain.

I like to have him think that I am always about to play some cruel prank upon him, such as tickling his ear with a straw or pricking him with a pin.

I greatly enjoy his little frowns and his efforts at self-preservation. I think they make him a hundred times more desirable and attractive.

After I have worried him as long as I wish, I change my tactics, beg his pardon, and the little, "That's all right," that he is *sure* to say, is the sweetest feature of all.

I do not care how rough or commanding he is with me as long as I am sure he is in fun, but the moment he assumes any felt superiority or right to command me, all is over between us.

It is impossible for me to have any sexual desire for a fleshy man without mustache. He is perfectly repulsive to me.

I was never attracted to anyone at first sight who had no mustache, but in a few instances, I have learned to love clean-shaven men.

Sometimes, when on the streets, I see a man walking from me who is just my ideal in form and carriage, and I cross the street or overtake him that I may see his face.

If he has no mustache, he is no more to me than a lamp post, and I never give him another glance or thought.

Fortunately, I have not for several years fallen in love with a boy, and I am sure I never shall again, for as I grow older, my aversion for clean-shaven faces increases.

I would not for anything tease or worry a small man with whom I am in love. To the contrary, I find it impossible to be as gentle with him as I wish to be.

If, by accident, I cause him pain, it hurts me more than it does him.

I completely forget myself and everything else in my desire to give him pleasure.

I like to place my hand on his ear and head, and lay my cheek so lightly against his own that he can scarcely feel it.

Placing my ear to his breast and listening to his heart, gives me the greatest pleasure.

To take his hand gently in my own, and close up his fist, finger by finger, is another one of my favorite modes of caressing a little man. I usually begin with his thumb, and end my work by placing a kiss upon his finger tips.

I like to pass my fingers through his hair, and twist or comb his mustache, taking every care not to hurt him.

I feel more real lust for large men, but I love the small ones far more dearly.

A physical deficiency, as a missing eye, finger or limb, often increases my love for small men, but large ones must be perfect physically.

There is a little one-eyed man in this city whom I love so dearly that I can scarcely resist speaking to him on the streets.

We were in the same crowd once, but my great love for him made me timid, and I did not address him.

He is a perfect little Apollo from head to foot, but I am sure I should never have loved him so if he had two good eyes.

There is also a physician in St. Louis whose physical shortcoming has caused me to love him devotedly, yet I have never spoken to him.

For several months I met him on the streets every morning as I went to my work, and oh, how I longed to put my arms around him and tell him how I loved him and how sorry I was for him!

All the loves to which I now refer are of a lustful nature, softened and beautified by sympathy, and they are the sweetest of all passionate love.

I am never attracted in a lustful way to a sickly man or one deformed from birth. The only love I could ever feel for such would be purely sweet and spiritual in its nature.

A man (or what the surgeon has left of him) must be what I call perfectly formed if I love him passionately.

Bow legs, stooped shoulders, knocked knees, etc., are a death blow to my passions.

The walk, dress, and disposition of a man influence me greatly.

He may be a perfect model of perfection in face and form, but if he is effeminate or affected in any way, I cannot endure him.

I like to see a man neat and clean always, but an over-dressed man disgusts rather than pleases me. I do not remember ever to have been attracted to a man who wore a silk hat and evening dress.

I have a friend in the city who wears, during the day, a neat but inexpensive business suit, and a little soft hat, and when I see him thus attired, I love him most passionately; but when he appears in his evening suit, silk hat, with eye-glass, walking-cane, and aristocratic airs, I can't tolerate him.

I have a great dislike for any other than a sack coat, and if I first see a frock [coat], I rarely ever glance at the face of the wearer.

This has been a great safeguard against my falling in love with ministers.

A handsome man in blue overalls, if they are worn to protect a better suit, is most attractive to me.

While I shrink from filth and rags, the well-dressed man is not my ideal from a lustful point of view.

I don't mind if a man is educated and refined, if he seeks to make no show of either, but I am much more apt to fall in love with the uneducated laborer, if he is entirely unassuming; but an ignorant man trying to appear well-informed is unbearable.

I know a man who "fills the bill" perfectly.

He weighs about 185 pounds, is 6 feet tall, perfectly formed and proportioned, has a nice mustache, and knows exactly how to dress.

He never wears anything showy or loud, and every article of his clothing is chosen with an eye to his own comfort.

When he walks, there is not a superfluous motion about his body.

His manly voice and manner are perfectly natural.

He is not educated, and never makes the least attempt to appear so.

He talks but little, always using the very simplest words that will convey his thoughts.

His hands are very hard and full of corns, which he neither attempts to display nor conceal.

Everything about him seems to say, "Here I am, just as I am. If you like me, all right; if not, then leave me alone."

He is a man of whom I would never tire.

He is gentle and affectionate, without being soft and silly; very passionate, but never coarse and brutal.

He is self-forgetful in his regard for others, but never fawning in his attentions, and last, but not least, he knows exactly how often and how long to make his visits.

Art in a man must be so skillfully concealed in itself that I cannot detect it, otherwise I do not like him for any great length of time.

I am often made to love or dislike a man by some article of clothing, or a trivial act.

I have in mind an old man over sixty years of age, with whom I fell passionately in love because he wore a certain kind of shoes, and stood every evening in front of his saloon, holding, with his right hand, the rope that supported his awnings.

This was a favorite position of his while talking to his friends.

A shoe that is out of style disgusts me with the wearer, unless it is worn for comfort; then it is all right; but a pointed toe, worn now, at once cools my desire.

I think there is nothing half so beautiful as a well-formed man in his underwear, but if he dares to undresss entirely in my presence, I never can tolerate him again.

Coarse, vulgar language has almost the same effect upon me.

I am wholly indifferent as to a man's sexual development if he is normal.

If I fall in love with a man, and afterwards learn that he is married, my passion wanes at once, and usually dies entirely.

I, of course, have a great aversion for women in a lustful way, and look upon a man's raving over them as the greatest of all weakness, absolutely incomprehensible to me.

I never fall in love with street-car men, because they wear caps, that style of which repels me.

I do not usually care for uniforms especially, but a policeman's blue coat, brass buttons, and quaint hat fill me with lustful longing.

Besides my sexual perversions, there are many other peculiarities which distinguish me from the natural man.

I have no sense of direction whatever, and when in a strange town, I must carefully watch the numbers of the streets and often make inquiries that I may not lose my way.

Frequently, when I come out of a building, it seems to have changed to the opposite side of the street, and it is then that I always lose my way if I am not very careful.

Sometimes, while walking along the sidewalk, the whole city will suddenly turn around, and I will feel that I am going the wrong way; then I must again look out for numbers, and once finding east, I can easily find the other directions by a little rule I learned when a child in school.

Often, when in a great hurry, I rush on without thinking of the numbers, and finally open my eyes to the fact that I have gone many blocks in the wrong direction.

This is one of the most inconvenient deficiencies I have, but I see no cure for it.

I am at times filled with very peculiar desires, for which I cannot account.

A run-away team, or the passing of the hook and ladder and the hose wagon, have no effect upon me whatever; but when I see the horses dashing by with the engine, on their way to a fire, a feeling of indescribably wild and rapturously keen delight thrills my being from head to foot.

I involuntarily clench my fists till my nails almost cut my palms, and I feel that I should like to spring in their way and be crushed into a million atoms.

I don't think I shall ever do so, however, for my reason never deserts me; and now, since my struggles have ended, and my mind is in a more restful state, the desire doesn't seem quite so intense.

Well, my story is about finished. Of course, I have not told all the events, impressions and desires with which my life has been filled, for I did not wish to tax my readers' patience unnecessarily.

I have endeavored to speak only of the characteristics which distinguish me from the natural man, omitting those common to the masses.

I have not spoken of my long and fierce battle with poverty from the age of seventeen to the present time, nor have I said much of the constant, vigilant and almost superhuman effort it requires to *be* one thing and to seem another for a whole lifetime.

I have not referred to the violent fits of jealousy that at times have almost driven me mad, for all these may be felt, in a measure, by the natural man; but the leading points I have presented as minutely as I deemed discreet.

Now, as a last appeal, I beg each and every reader of my little book to overlook its many defects and disgusting features; to accept it as a *truth* that *exists* regardless of its gravity; to think carefully over its contents, and try to devise some means of relief for the thousands whose sufferings are similar to my own; thus becoming a benefactor to society and a blessing to the world in which he lives.

END

Grey Fox Books of Particular Interest